CHALLENGER 4

ADULT READING SERIES

COREA MURPHY

NEW READERS PRESS
Publishing Division of Laubach Literacy International
Syracuse, New York

ISBN 0-88336-784-X

EACH ONE TEACH ONE

© 1985
New Readers Press
Publishing Division of Laubach Literacy International
Box 131, Syracuse, New York 13210

Printed in the United States of America

Designed by Chris Steenwerth
Cover by Chris Steenwerth

Cover photo by Gerard Fritz

20   19   18   17   16

About the Author

Corea Murphy has worked in the field of education since the early 1960s. In addition to classroom and tutorial teaching, Ms. Murphy has developed language arts curriculum guides for public high schools, conducted curriculum and effectiveness workshops, and established an educational program for residents in a drug rehabilitation facility.

Ms. Murphy became interested in creating a reading series for older students when she began working with adults and adolescents in the early 1970s. The **Challenger Adult Reading Series** is the result of her work with these students.

In a very real sense, the students contributed greatly to the development of this reading series. Their enthusiasm for learning to read and their willingness to work hard provided inspiration, and their many helpful suggestions influenced the content of both the student books and the teacher's manuals.

It is to these students that the **Challenger Adult Reading Series** is dedicated with the hope that others who wish to become good readers will find this reading program both helpful and stimulating.

A special note of gratitude is also extended to Kay Koschnick, Christina Jagger, and Mary Hutchison of New Readers Press for their work and support in guiding this series to completion.

Table of Contents

Lesson 1

The Heart

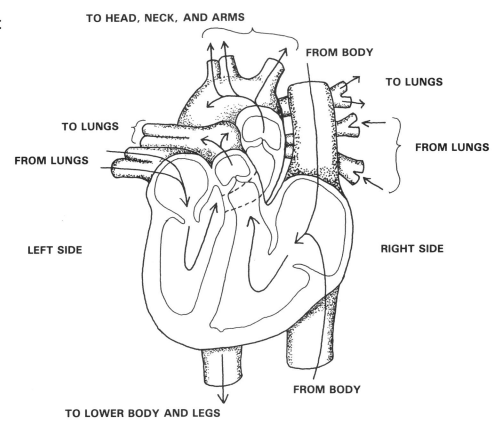

TO HEAD, NECK, AND ARMS

FROM BODY

TO LUNGS

TO LUNGS

FROM LUNGS

FROM LUNGS

LEFT SIDE

RIGHT SIDE

FROM BODY

TO LOWER BODY AND LEGS

Words for Study

performs	inches	disease	carbon dioxide
collects	normal	located	messages
veins	normally	upper	stomp
arteries	oxygen	actions	toes

The Heart

Day after day, the heart pumps blood throughout your body. Its beat goes on and on with very little help from you. The heart beats, or pumps, five quarts of blood throughout the body in about sixty seconds. In just one year, the heart pumps enough blood to fill from 97 to 200 tank cars with 8,000 gallons each!

The heart is really two pumps in one. Each side of the heart performs a different pumping job. The right side takes blood from the body and pumps it into the lungs. The left side collects blood from the lungs and then pumps it to the body. It is the job of the veins in the body to bring the blood back into the heart. Arteries, on the other hand, carry blood from the heart to all parts of the body.

Your heart does enough work in just one hour to lift a weight of 1½ tons more than one foot off the ground; yet it is only about the size of your fist. In grownups, the heart is about five inches long, three and one-half inches wide, and two and one-half inches thick. A man's heart weighs about eleven ounces. A woman's heart weighs about nine ounces. The heart lies near the middle of the chest toward the front. The lower end of the heart is the part that you feel beating.

A person's heart normally beats about 70 to 80 times a minute, but the rate changes in order to give the body as much oxygen as it needs. For example, your heart beats much faster when you exercise. It is rushing more oxygen to your body by speeding up the flow of blood.

There are many other examples of how the heart changes its rate of beating to meet a certain need. When you become angry, afraid, or excited, your heart beats harder and faster. This is one of the reasons why being angry or upset a lot is unhealthy; it is just too hard on your heart. However, it seems that many people in the United States do not know how important it is to live calm and peaceful lives because 1,660,000 people die from heart disease every year.

1 **About the Reading.** Answer these questions.

1. True or false? Write *true* if the sentence is true. Write *false* if the sentence is false.

_____ a. A person's heart normally beats about seventy to eighty times a minute.

_____ b. A woman's heart is larger than a man's heart.

_____ c. Each side of the heart has a different job.

_____ d. The heart beats five quarts of blood throughout the body in about sixty minutes.

_____ e. The heart is about the size of your fist.

_____ f. The heart is located on the left side of the chest.

_____ g. The heart is really two pumps.

_____ h. The heart is working harder when you are playing sports.

_____ i. The upper end of the heart is the part you feel beating.

_____ j. When the heart beats fast, it sends less oxygen to the body.

2. Explain how a person who gets angry a lot is hurting his health.

_____

_____

3. How many people in the United States die from heart disease every year?

_____

What do you think?

4. Do you think that people would lose their tempers less often if they knew how much this hurt their health? Be sure to explain your answer.

_____

_____

2 **The Human Body.** Match the words on the left to the sentences on the right.

artery

bloodstream

brain

elbow

lungs

nerve

nose

ribs

spleen

vein

_____ 1. This carries blood away from the heart.

_____ 2. This carries blood to the heart.

_____ 3. This contains the sense of smell and is used for inhaling air.

_____ 4. This controls many of your body actions and is the place in which thinking happens.

_____ 5. This is the joint between the lower and the upper arm.

_____ 6. This is the stream of blood flowing through a living body.

_____ 7. This sends messages from one part of the body to another.

_____ 8. These are twelve pairs of long, curved bones that extend from the spine.

_____ 9. These take carbon dioxide from the blood and give oxygen to it. (You have two of them.)

_____ 10. This works as a blood filter and stores blood.

3 **The Ending -er.** Add -er to the words listed below. Study the examples before you begin.

1. deal   _dealer_

2. read   _____

3. blend   _____

4. print   _____

5. perform _____

1. trade   _trader_

2. shake   _____

3. hike   _____

4. line   _____

5. believe _____

1. run   _runner_

2. drum   _____

3. bid   _____

4. flip   _____

5. pat   _____

4 **Syllables.** Each of the words listed below has two syllables. Write these two syllables on the lines to the right of the word. If a vowel is underlined, mark it either long or short. Study the examples before you begin.

1. bookcase   _book_ • _cāse_
2. winner   _wĭn_ • _ner_
3. strongly   _____ • _____
4. clutter   _____ • _____
5. locate   _____ • _____
6. hopeless   _____ • _____
7. normal   _____ • _____
8. forgive   _____ • _____
9. copper   _____ • _____
10. perform   _____ • _____

5 **Brain Benders.** Each of these common sayings mentions a part of the body. Choose the answer that best explains each saying and write it on the line. If you've never heard the saying before, get a friend to help you or make a good guess.

1. If "your heart is in the right place," you're _____
    (a) healthy.
    (b) kind.
    (c) like everybody else.
    (d) normal.

2. If you "set your heart on something," you _____
    (a) fall in love.
    (b) hug somebody.
    (c) lie down.
    (d) want something badly.

3. A person who "looks down his nose" at somebody else is _____
    (a) a snob.
    (b) crude.
    (c) friendly.
    (d) tall.

4. When something "goes to your head," you're _____

   (a) full of pride.
   (b) tense.
   (c) thinking.
   (d) unhappy.

5. When you have a "lump in your throat," you feel _____

   (a) bored.
   (b) calm.
   (c) sick.
   (d) strongly moved.

6. When you see things "eye to eye" with a friend, you _____

   (a) agree with your friend.
   (b) are the same height.
   (c) disagree.
   (d) don't wear glasses.

7. If you "put your foot down," you _____

   (a) are walking.
   (b) have a cramp.
   (c) insist on having your own way.
   (d) stomp around.

8. When somebody "pulls your leg," he is _____

   (a) fighting you.
   (b) hitting you.
   (c) hurting you.
   (d) teasing you.

9. If a person "steps on your toes," he _____

   (a) hurts your feelings.
   (b) hurts your feet.
   (c) isn't watching where he's going.
   (d) says that he's sorry.

10. If something makes your "blood boil," you are _____

   (a) angry.
   (b) confused.
   (c) lively.
   (d) relaxed.

Lesson 2

Babe Ruth

National Baseball Library

Words for Study

Babe	American	Sox	built
Herman	league	mound	paddle
Bambino	Yankees	polo	racket
hero	Baltimore	stadium	tennis

Babe Ruth

George Herman Ruth (1895-1948) had many nicknames including "Babe," "Bambino," and "the Home Run King." Even though he was a hero to millions of people, he certainly didn't live the way many people thought heroes should live. For example, the president of the American League, who really respected Ruth's skill as a baseball player, was once quoted as saying, "Ruth has the mind of a fifteen-year-old."

The New York Yankees tried many different ways to get Ruth to act more like a hero. They chewed him out, benched him, and fined him. However, nothing worked. Ruth loved to have a good time, and he liked everything that a dollar could buy.

Babe Ruth grew up in the streets of Baltimore. His mother and father either didn't want him or didn't know what to do with him, so they sent him to reform school in 1902 when Ruth was seven years old. The only time Ruth seemed at peace with himself was when he was pitching a ball or knocking the cover off it with a bat.

When Ruth was nineteen years old, the Boston Red Sox paid $2,900 for his contract. When the manager saw how Ruth hit, he moved him from the pitching mound to the outfield so he could play every day. This scheme paid off. In 1919, Ruth hit twenty-nine home runs, a new record in baseball.

The New York Yankees were so impressed with Ruth's hitting that they spent $125,000 to bring him to New York. It was worth it. Ruth hit fifty-four home runs for the Yankees in 1920 and fifty-nine the next year. Babe's bat brought so many fans into the rented polo grounds that the Yankees decided to build their own park. This is why Yankee Stadium is called "The House that Ruth Built." In 1927, Babe Ruth broke his own record and hit sixty home runs.

Ruth spent the money he made as fast as he earned it. One season he made $40,000; yet a friend had to lend him money so he could get to training camp the next spring. Another time, he lost $35,000 on a single horse race.

Even when Babe Ruth's legs gave out, and the Yankees traded him after he had played with them for fifteen years, the fans stayed with him. When he died of cancer in 1948, eighty thousand people filed into Yankee Stadium to pay respect to their hero.

Adapted from *Babe: The Legend Comes to Life.* Copyright © 1974 by Robert W. Creamer. Reprinted by permission of Simon & Schuster, Inc. and Sterling Lord Literistic, Inc.

1 **About the Reading.** Answer these questions.

1. In what city did Babe Ruth grow up? _____

2. In what kind of place did he grow up? _____

3. What was the name of the first team for which Babe Ruth played? _____

4. What is "The House that Ruth Built"? _____

5. How long did Babe Ruth play for the New York Yankees? _____

6. Why did the Yankees trade Babe Ruth?

_____

7. What was the cause of Babe Ruth's death? _____

8. How old was Babe Ruth when he died? _____

9. Explain why some people thought that Babe Ruth didn't live the way a hero should live.

_____

_____

2 **Games and Sports.** Write the word on the line to the right that has nothing to do with the game or sport listed at the beginning of the row. Get a friend to help with the ones that give you trouble.

1. **baseball:**	quarterback	catcher	infield	bunt	_____
2. **football:**	outfield	guard	coach	pass	_____
3. **basketball:**	overtime	height	court	yards	_____
4. **bowling:**	strikes	pins	spares	bases	_____
5. **boxing:**	ringside	rounds	squares	trunks	_____
6. **swimming:**	breast stroke	height	laps	ocean	_____
7. **ping-pong:**	paddle	racket	serve	table	_____
8. **tennis:**	racket	paddle	net	serve	_____
9. **chess:**	checkers	check	pawn	queen	_____
10. **poker:**	royal flush	dice	bet	straight	_____

3 **Words That Mean the Same.** Match each word at the left with the word that has the same meaning.

brag
car
conceal
female
gloomy
message
normal
perform
trousers
wrong

_____ 1. act

_____ 2. automobile

_____ 3. boast

_____ 4. common

_____ 5. downhearted

_____ 6. hide

_____ 7. mistaken

_____ 8. note

_____ 9. slacks

_____ 10. woman

4 **Word Opposites.** Match each word at the left with the word that means the opposite.

brand-new

built

conclude   _____   1. begin

dull   _____   2. center

edge

increase   _____   3. destroyed

normal   _____   4. gleaming

plump

restless   _____   5. odd

smooth   _____   6. reduce

                  _____   7. relaxed

                  _____   8. rough

                  _____   9. skinny

                  _____   10. used

5 **More Work with the Ending -er.** Add -er to the words listed below. Study the examples before you begin.

1. buzz _buzzer_   1. wipe _wiper_   1. dig _digger_

2. jump _____   2. inside _____   2. gun _____

3. kill _____   3. outside _____   3. log _____

4. learn _____   4. invade _____   4. jog _____

5. broil _____   5. tune _____   5. skip _____

6. strain _____   6. breathe _____   6. snap _____

6 **Syllables.** Each of the words listed below has two syllables. Write these two syllables on the lines to the right of the word. If a vowel is underlined, mark it either long or short.

1. gr<u>a</u>veyard   _____ • _____

2. d<u>i</u>sturb   _____ • _____

3. wr<u>a</u>pper   _____ • _____

4. <u>i</u>nqu<u>i</u>re   _____ • _____

5. <u>u</u>nd<u>i</u>d   _____ • _____

6. t<u>e</u>nn<u>i</u>s   _____ • _____

7. br<u>e</u>akfast   _____ • _____

8. f<u>i</u>ddle   _____ • _____

9. p<u>a</u>ddle   _____ • _____

10. tr<u>a</u>ining   _____ • _____

Lesson 3

Time

Words for Study

concept	museum	Indians	holidays
likely	object	Southwest	borrowed
chat	prompt	strolled	steal
Asia	Pueblo	half-hour	shortcut

Time

A concept is a thought or an idea about something. Most of our concepts about time come from the place in which we live. For example, in the United States, different parts of the day have certain meanings. Americans don't tend to visit or call their friends very early in the morning or very late at night. Thus, if you do phone or drop in on a friend during either of these times, it is likely to be taken as a matter of life and death. However, there are countries in which people do drop by at two or three o'clock in the morning just to chat, and they don't find this strange at all.

Also, to Americans, a "long time" can mean almost anything—ten or twenty years, two or three months, a few weeks, or even a few days. In South Asia, however, the people think that a "long time" means at least thousands of years. They think time is like a huge museum with many, many halls and little rooms. They believe that each of us walks through this museum in the dark, holding a light so we can see each painting or object. The museum belongs to God, and the people in South Asia think that only He knows all that is in this museum.

A third concept that most Americans have about time is that people should be prompt. If an American is not prompt for work or meetings, he is often looked at as being rude or unfit for his job.

However, even within the borders of the United States, there are people who do not think being prompt is important at all. For the Pueblo Indians, who live in the American Southwest, things begin when the time is ripe and no sooner. Once, a man drove forty-five miles over bumpy roads to get to a Christmas dance that some Pueblo Indians were having. When he arrived at the church where the dance was to be held, all he found were a few white townspeople who were wondering when the dance would start. Then a few Pueblo Indians strolled into the church. They had no idea when the dance was going to start either. In fact, they didn't even seem to care.

At last, at two o'clock in the morning, when the white people were nearly exhausted from the cold and the waiting, the deep sounds of the drums burst upon the quiet night. Without warning, the dance had begun.

Adapted from *The Silent Language* by Edward T. Hall. Copyright © 1959 by Edward T. Hall. Reprinted by permission of author and Doubleday & Co., Inc.

1 **About the Reading.** Answer these questions.

1. Define the word *concept*.

_____

2. How do most Americans react if they get a phone call at two o'clock in the morning?

_____

3. What do Americans think is "a long time"?

_____

4. How do people in South Asia define "a long time"?

_____

5. What do many Americans think about a person who is not prompt?

_____

6. When do the Pueblo Indians decide to begin something?

_____

7. Describe what happened to the man who went to the Pueblo Indians' Christmas dance.

_____

_____

8. The main idea about this reading is that _____

_____

   (a) time is like a huge museum.
   (b) different groups of people have different concepts of time.
   (c) people should be prompt.
   (d) many Americans go to bed earlier than people living in other countries.

What do you think?

9. What is "a long time" to you?

_____

_____

2 **Time.** Use the sets of words at the left to answer these questions. Study the example before you begin.

1. Write the seasons of the year in order.

autumn
spring
summer
winter

a. _Spring_

b. _Summer_

c. _autumn_

d. _winter_

2. Write these days of the week in the right order.

Friday
Thursday
Tuesday
Wednesday

a. _____

b. _____

c. _____

d. _____

3. Write these times of the day in the right order.

dawn
dusk
midnight
noon

a. _____

b. _____

c. _____

d. _____

4. Write these holidays in the right order.

Christmas Eve
Easter
Fourth of July
New Year's Day

a. _____

b. _____

c. _____

d. _____

5. Write these times in order from the smallest to the largest.

half-hour
hour
minute
second

a. _____

b. _____

c. _____

d. _____

6. Write these months of the year in the right order.

August
July
October
September

a. _____

b. _____

c. _____

d. _____

7. Write these times in order from the shortest to the longest.

day
month
week
year

a. _____

b. _____

c. _____

d. _____

8. Write these in order from the smallest to the largest.

alarm clock
grandfather's clock
sun
wristwatch

a. _____

b. _____

c. _____

d. _____

9. Write these times in order from the one that gives you the least money at work to the one that gives you the most.

a normal working day
double time
free time
time and a half

a. _____

b. _____

c. _____

d. _____

3 **More about Time.** Many Americans talk about time as if it were money. Use the words at the left to complete these sentences about Mr. Rush. Take your time!

blown
borrowed
earned
lend
lost
save
spent
steal
use
waste

1. When the alarm clock rang, Mr. Rush turned it off and rolled over in his bed to _____ an extra fifteen minutes of sleep.

2. He felt that he had _____ this extra time because he had been up until after midnight writing a report.

3. Then, because Mr. Rush was late, he thought he could _____ some time by driving to work instead of taking the bus.

4. He didn't want to _____ one minute, so he took a shortcut through the city park.

5. He would _____ the time he had saved to complete the report that his boss wanted on his desk by noon.

6. However, Mr. Rush got lost taking the shortcut, and he _____ twenty minutes trying to find someone who could tell him how to get out of the park.

7. He _____ another thirty minutes when he ran over a nail and got a flat tire.

8. Since he had _____ the morning anyway, Mr. Rush decided to stop at a nearby coffee shop and have doughnuts and coffee.

9. The woman behind the counter asked Mr. Rush if he could _____ her ten minutes of his time to help move the candy machine.

10. Mr. Rush smiled sadly and told her, "I'm sorry, but I have a bad heart. In fact, my doctor thought I'd be dead six months ago, so I guess you could say I'm living on _____ time."

4 **The Ending -y.** Add -y to the words listed below. Study the examples before you begin.

1. soap _Soapy_
2. dust _____
3. sand _____
4. curl _____
5. bush _____

1. breeze _breezy_
2. wheeze _____
3. scare _____
4. nerve _____
5. grease _____

1. pep _peppy_
2. pot _____
3. fat _____
4. chop _____
5. clam _____

5 **Syllables.** Each of these words has two syllables. Write these two syllables on the lines to the right of the word. If a vowel is underlined, mark it either long or short.

1. wristwatch   _____ • _____

2. Southwest   _____ • _____

3. clammy   _____ • _____

4. shortcut   _____ • _____

5. object   _____ • _____

6. breathless   _____ • _____

7. require   _____ • _____

8. sadness   _____ • _____

9. hopeful   _____ • _____

10. mistrust   _____ • _____

Lesson 4

Insects

Can you tell which of these are insects and which are not? See page 27 for answers.

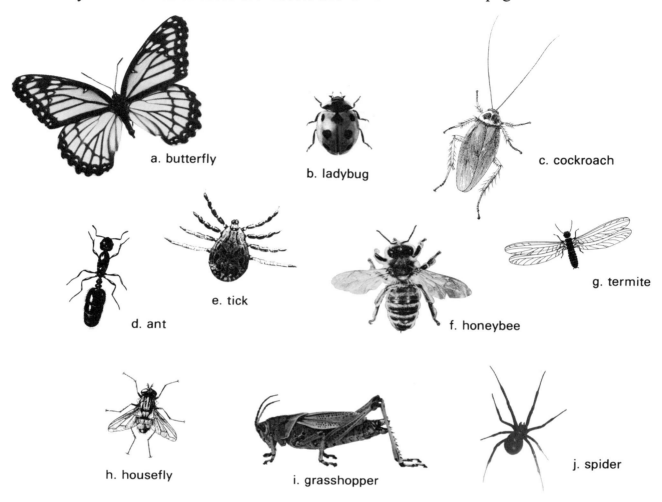

a. butterfly

b. ladybug

c. cockroach

d. ant

e. tick

f. honeybee

g. termite

h. housefly

i. grasshopper

j. spider

Words for Study

picnics	deserts	feelers	ladybug
forests	meadows	degrees	termite
pollen	swamps	spider	orange
amount	tiny	butterfly	color
total	mouthparts	grasshopper	latch

Insects

Most of us think of insects as something that should be destroyed. Some bite. Some sting. Some carry diseases. Others mess up picnics, invade kitchens, or get into clothes. Still others destroy crops, spoil fruits, or kill trees. Each year, insects do twice as much harm to the forests as fires do.

Yet this would be a poor world without insects. Insects are food for birds and bats, fish and frogs, and even for other insects. Many insects return matter to the soil which helps new life to form. Insects give us such things as wax, honey, and silk. But the insects' greatest gift is that they help plants to grow. In their search for food, many insects carry pollen from one flower to another which increases the amount of seeds and fruits.

There are so many kinds of insects in the world that, even if you learned the names of one hundred insects every day, you would still need more than twenty years to learn all the known insects. So far, people who study insects have named more than 800,000 different kinds. There may be ten times more than this number of insects that have not yet been named. There are more than twice as many kinds of insects as the total number of kinds of all other living things— both plants and animals.

Insects are found over almost all the earth. They can live in deserts, hot springs, snow fields, and caves. They can live in ponds and swift rivers, in forests, meadows, and swamps. Only salt water seems to stop insects in their tracks. There are very few insects that can live in the ocean.

Not every tiny thing that crawls or hops is an insect. If you're not certain, count the legs. If there are six legs, it's an insect. If there are more or less than six legs, it's something else.

The body of all insects has three parts. First comes the head with eyes, mouthparts, and "feelers," which are used for hearing, smelling, and tasting. Insects have no necks. The head is joined to the middle part of the body. All six legs and the wings, if they have any, are joined to this middle part. The last part of the insect's body is for taking care of food and laying eggs.

Insects are cold-blooded animals. When it is hot, an insect can move very quickly; but when it is cold, it becomes more and more tired. Insects cannot fly when it is below 50 degrees F., and insects that live in the north must stay in sheltered places throughout the winter.

So, if you are the kind of person who is afraid of spiders or hates flies, you'd better move to a place where it's always winter!

Adapted from *Insects from Close Up* by Eleanor Fanning. Copyright © 1965 by Thomas J. Crowell.

1 **About the Reading.** Answer these questions.

1. How many known kinds of insects are there? _____

2. Name the one place where insects have trouble living. _____

3. How can you tell if something tiny is an insect?

_____

4. How many parts does an insect's body have? _____

5. What does the insect use for hearing, smelling, and tasting? _____

6. What is the insect's greatest gift?

_____

7. List three other ways that explain how insects are helpful.

a. _____

b. _____

c. _____

8. List six reasons that explain why most people hate insects.

a. _____   d. _____

b. _____   e. _____

c. _____   f. _____

9. Why would it be a good idea to live in a cold place if you hate insects?

_____

What do you think?

10. Based on what you learned about how many insects there are in the world, why is it a good thing for people that insects are so tiny?

_____

2 **Name That Insect or Bug.** Match each word at the left with the sentence that best describes it.

ants
bee
butterfly
cockroach
grasshopper
housefly
ladybug
spider
termite
tick

_____

_____

_____

_____

_____

_____

_____

_____

_____

_____

1. The Indians call this "white man's fly." It lives in a hive and makes honey.

2. This is sometimes called a "white ant" even though it has nothing in common with an ant. It lives in and eats wood.

3. This has bright orange colors and may have up to nineteen black spots.

4. This traps an insect in its loose web.

5. This likes to latch onto dogs or people because it needs blood in order to stay alive.

6. This does not bite, but it does spread disease. You see a lot of them buzzing around when the weather is warm.

7. This is a beautiful insect that some people enjoy catching in nets.

8. This has strong hind legs which help it jump.

9. There are more of these than any other kind of insect. The kind we find in our kitchens is often crawling around the sugar.

10. This insect has been around for more than three hundred million years. Once it gets into your house, it is hard to get rid of.

3 **Which Word Fits Best?** Choose the right word from the four choices and put it on the line.

1. Termite is to wood as _____ is to blood.
   (a) grasshopper   (b) honeybee   (c) ladybug   (d) tick

2. Ant is to whale as tiny is to _____.
   (a) huge   (b) insect   (c) warm-blooded   (d) water

3. Fresh water is to river as salt water is to _____.
   (a) lake   (b) ocean   (c) pond   (d) stream

4. Hundred is to number as _____ is to color.
   (a) bright   (b) dull   (c) orange   (d) pear

5. Spider is to insect as whale is to _____.
   (a) animal   (b) fish   (c) mammal   (d) ocean

6. Shelter is to harm as _____ is to upset.
   (a) comfort   (b) command   (c) compete   (d) complain

7. Grass is to meadow as _____ is to pond.
   (a) deep   (b) fish   (c) insects   (d) water

8. Forest is to trees as desert is to _____.
   (a) heat   (b) sand   (c) tents   (d) woods

4 **More Work with the Ending -y.** Add -y to the words listed below. Study the examples before you begin.

1. speed _speedy_   1. choose _choosy_   1. bag _baggy_

2. rust _____   2. scale _____   2. Tom _____

3. silk _____   3. sponge _____ 3. gum _____

4. cream _____ 4. paste _____   4. smog _____

5. leaf _____   5. mouse _____   5. flop _____

6. flower _____ 6. bone _____   6. slop _____

5 **Syllables.** Each of these words has two syllables. Write these syllables on the lines to the right of the word. If a vowel is underlined, mark it either long or short.

1. cockro͟ach   _____ • _____

2. pic͟nic   _____ • _____

3. term͟ite   _____ • _____

4. mouthpart   _____ • _____

5. i͟nsect   _____ • _____

6. po͟llen   _____ • _____

7. flo͟ppy   _____ • _____

8. co͟ncept   _____ • _____

9. outlook   _____ • _____

10. u͟nle͟ss   _____ • _____

Answers to quiz on page 22:

a. insect   b. insect   c. insect   d. insect   e. not an insect

f. insect   g. insect   h. insect   i. insect   j. not an insect

Lesson 5

The Brain Sees All

Words for Study

per	nevertheless	one-fourth	yellow
flicker	one-third	unaware	menu
effect	affect	watcher	program
aware	intermission	dial	channel

The Brain Sees All

When you watch television, you may think you're looking at a picture, but you really aren't. What you see on a television screen are three hundred thousand tiny, glowing dots. There is no picture at all!

These dots seem to be lit all the time; but in fact, they are not. All the dots go off thirty times per second, giving what is known as the flicker effect. This flickering happens so fast that our minds are not aware of it. Nevertheless, studies have shown that, although our minds are not aware of the flickering, our bodies are very much aware of it. The cells in our brains record *all* these dots (remember, they go off thirty times per second), but our minds are able to make sense out of only ten of these thirty times.

What this means is that whenever you watch television, or even a movie, you are aware of only one-third of what you're seeing. How can this affect you? Some years ago, a study was made of people who were watching a movie. The people didn't know it, but the words EAT POPCORN were flashing on and off the screen while the movie was going on. These two words were flashing so fast that the people's minds could not tell this was happening. All they were aware of was that they were watching a movie.

However, the brain, as we said before, records everything, and the cells of the brain recorded every single EAT POPCORN sign that flashed on the screen. Sure enough, during intermission nearly everybody rushed out to the lobby to buy popcorn. Even people who normally never bought popcorn stood in line to buy a box. Based on this one example, can you see how strongly you can be affected by watching television or a movie and not even know it?

1   **About the Reading.** Answer these questions.

1. When you watch television, you are really looking at _____.

    (a) a movie   (b) a picture   (c) dots   (d) nothing at all

2. Our minds can see only _____ of these flickerings on the television screen per second.

    (a) 300,000   (b) ten   (c) thirteen   (d) thirty

3. When you watch a movie or television, you really see only _____ of what's happening.

    (a) all   (b) one-fourth   (c) one-half   (d) one-third

4. The EAT POPCORN study shows that people _____

    (a) can be unaware of what's happening.
    (b) hate popcorn.
    (c) love popcorn.
    (d) hated the movie.

5. The _____ records everything that happens.

    (a) brain   (b) mind   (c) newspaper   (d) watcher

6. A main idea of this reading is that _____

_____

    (a) watching television is a relaxing way to pass the time.
    (b) watching television is not a good way to pass the time.
    (c) we can be affected by things that we're not even aware of.
    (d) people can be forced to eat popcorn.

What do you think?

7. Why do you think ads such as the "eat popcorn" ad are against the law?

_____

_____

8. Do you think ads affect how people spend their money when they go shopping?

_____

2 **Putting Sentences in Order.** Mrs. Woods has decided to watch a certain program on television. Put the steps she takes in the right order on the lines below the sentences.

She checks the *TV Guide* to see what time the program is on.
She falls asleep on the couch.
She also reads what channel the program is on.
She plays with the knobs to get a better picture.
She turns on the set.
She turns the knob to the right channel.
The picture is not clear at all.
The program turns out to be very dull.

1. _____

2. _____

3. _____

4. _____

5. _____

6. _____

7. _____

8. _____

3 **Syllables.** Each of the words listed below has *three* syllables. Write these syllables on the lines to the right of each word.

1. outstanding   _____ • _____ • _____

2. underground   _____ • _____ • _____

3. yesterday   _____ • _____ • _____

4. butterfly   _____ • _____ • _____

5. Washington   _____ • _____ • _____

6. commandment   _____ • _____ • _____

7. grasshopper   _____ • _____ • _____

8. performer   _____ • _____ • _____

9. remember   _____ • _____ • _____

10. apartment   _____ • _____ • _____

4 **Working with Headings.** It is said that most Americans spend at least four hours each day watching television. What else could we be doing during this time? Match the headings with the word groups that describe something else people can do during their spare time. Study the example before you begin.

Cooking
Going out for Dinner
Going to a Concert
Going to Night School
Hiking
Making Things
Playing Ball
Reading
✓ Spending Time with Friends
Talking on the Phone

Spending Time with Friends
    going places
    laughing
    listening
    talking

book	boots	bat
newspaper	fresh air	home run
short story	outdoors	mitt
sports page	trails	second base

pots and pans	dial tone	blackboard
recipes	number	chalk
stove	phone book	classroom
tablespoon	yellow pages	teacher

boards	band	menu
hammer	drums	order
nails	piano	tip
saw	singer	waiter

5 **Words That End in -y.** Sound out the words at the left. Some of the vowels have been marked to help you. Then use these words to complete the sentences.

băttery
belly
brăndy
bully
bŭnny
cooky
grāvy
moody
mŭggy
pănty

1. Jill knew it was useless, but she asked her aunt if she could have just one

   oatmeal _____ before dinner anyway.

2. Eddie was happy to find a huge chocolate _____ in his Easter basket, but he had hoped for a real one.

3. Mrs. Carpenter bought six pairs of _____ hose at the store's going-out-of-business sale.

4. Paul asked his neighbor if he would help him charge his _____, so he could start the car.

5. The pain in his _____ got so bad that Matthew decided he had better see a doctor.

6. It was just too _____ to mow the lawn, so Sandy spent the afternoon sitting in front of the fan with a good book.

7. When June and John decided to get married, they went downtown to celebrate

   over a glass of _____.

8. Kirk had been so _____ for the past few weeks that his friends couldn't think of anything to do that would cheer him up.

9. Harvey was such a _____ on the school playground that the other children were afraid to play with him.

10. Tony couldn't stand mashed potatoes unless they were covered

    with _____.

Review: Lessons 1-5

1 **Answer These Questions.** Fill in the blanks with the right answers.

_____ 1. Is blood carried to the heart by an artery or a vein?

_____ 2. Is blood carried away from the heart by an artery or a vein?

_____ 3. Is *Pueblo* the name of an Indian or a Yankee?

_____ 4. Is *Babe Ruth* the name of an Indian or a Yankee?

_____ 5. Is a place where it is very wet likely to be called a desert or a swamp?

_____ 6. Is a place where it is very dry likely to be called a desert or a swamp?

_____ 7. Is the insect that eats wood called a termite or a grasshopper?

_____ 8. Is the insect that is known for its jumping skill called a grasshopper or a butterfly?

_____ 9. Do animals inhale carbon dioxide or oxygen?

_____ 10. Do animals exhale carbon dioxide or oxygen?

2 **Word Study.** Choose the right answer from the four choices and write it on the line.

_____ 1. If a light is flickering, it is _____.
(a) bright   (b) dirty   (c) dull   (d) going on and off

_____ 2. One-fourth of a dollar is _____.
(a) a dime   (b) a penny   (c) a quarter   (d) fifty cents

_____ 3. A person who is looked up to for the great things he has done is called a _____.
(a) bigwig   (b) hero   (c) movie star   (d) president

_____ 4. An example of Answer 3, who served as the first president of the United States is _____.
(a) Babe Ruth   (c) George Washington
(b) George Washington Carver   (d) the Pueblo Indians

_____ 5. An example of a city is _____.
(a) Asia   (b) Baltimore   (c) California   (d) Egypt

6. An example of a country is _____.

    (a) Asia   (b) Baltimore   (c) California   (d) United States

7. Where would you be likely to use a racket?

    (a) museum   (c) stadium
    (b) polo grounds   (d) tennis courts

8. Where would you be likely to go for a picnic?

    (a) desert   (b) meadow   (c) stadium   (d) swamp

9. Where would you be likely to go to see paintings?

    (a) meeting   (b) museum   (c) paint store   (d) stadium

10. Where would you be likely to go to meet a Pueblo Indian?

    (a) Baltimore   (c) South Asia
    (b) New England   (d) the American Southwest

11. If something is very sticky, it is _____.

    (a) gummy   (b) mousy   (c) sloppy   (b) spongy

12. Which word best describes the first season of the year?

    (a) clammy   (b) flowery   (c) muggy   (d) smoggy

13. A person who has the lowdown on what is going on is an _____.

    (a) insider   (b) invader   (c) learner   (d) outsider

14. Who would most likely want to feel peppy?

    (a) a believer   (b) a jogger   (c) a printer   (d) a trader

15. Which of these is not a holiday?

    (a) Christmas   (c) Mother's Day
    (b) Fourth of July   (d) Thanksgiving

3 **Words That Mean the Same.** Match each word at the left with the word that has nearly the same meaning.

chat
concept
jogger
locate
meadow
message
perform
total
underneath
upper

_____ 1. act

_____ 2. below

_____ 3. field

_____ 4. find

_____ 5. higher

_____ 6. idea

_____ 7. note

_____ 8. runner

_____ 9. sum

_____ 10. talk

4 **Word Opposites.** Match each word at the left with the word that means the opposite.

aware
baggy
cause
disease
exhale
hero
prompt
scaly
straight
townspeople

_____ 1. bum

_____ 2. country folks

_____ 3. curly

_____ 4. effect

_____ 5. good health

_____ 6. inhale

_____ 7. late

_____ 8. smooth

_____ 9. tight

_____ 10. unaware

Word Index: Lessons 1-5

A
action
affect
American
amount
artery
Asia
aware

B
Babe
baggy
Baltimore
Bambino
battery
believer
belly
bidder
blender
borrow
boxing
brandy
breather
breezy
broiler
built
bully
bunny
bushy
butterfly
buzzer

C
carbon
carbon dioxide
Carver, G.W.
channel
chat
choosy
choppy
Christmas Eve
clammy
collect
color
concept
cooky
creamy
curly

D
dealer
degree
desert
dial
digger
disease
drummer
dusty

E
effect
exhale

F
fatty
feeler
flicker
flipper
floppy
flowery
forest

G
grasshopper
gravy
greasy
gummy
gunner

H
half-hour
hearing
Herman
hero
hiker
holiday

I
inch
Indian
insider
intermission
invader

J
jog
jogger
jumper

K
killer

L
ladybug
latch
leafy
league
learner
likely
liner
locate
logger

M
meadow
menu
message
moody
mound
mousy

mouthpart
muggy
museum

N
nervy
nevertheless
normal
normally

O
object
one-fourth
one-third
orange
outsider
oxygen

P
paddle
panty
pasty
patter
peppy
per
perform
performer
picnic
pollen
polo
potty
printer
program
prompt
Pueblo

Q

R
racket
reader
reading
runner
rusty

S
sandy
scaly
scary
shaker
shortcut
silky
skipper
slop
sloppy
smoggy
snapper
soapy
southwest

sox
speedy
spider
spongy
stadium
steal
stomp
strainer
stroll
swamp

T
tennis
termite
tiny
toe
Tommy
total
trader
training
tuner
TV

U
unaware
upper
used

V
vein

W
watcher
wheezy
wiper

X

Y
Yankee
yellow

Z

Lesson 6

The Sun

Words for Study

process	narrow	offer	compound
skyscraper	beam	god	whiskey
receives	rays	prayers	outline
billionth	worshipped	worry	sudden

The Sun

All life on Earth depends on the sun for heat and light. Life on Earth also depends on the sun for food because all living things—both plants and animals—are part of a process called a food chain. This food chain starts with green plants which make food with the help of sunlight. Since all animals eat either plants or other animals that eat plants, you can see why the sun is so important.

Many people who lived a long time ago understood how important the sun was, and they worshipped it as a god. They would offer prayers and gifts to their sun god so that he would be pleased and always shine his light upon them.

The sun is a star. Even though it is about ninety-three million miles away from us, the sun is closer to Earth than any other star. This is why it looks so big and bright. There are stars that are 1,000 times larger than the sun, but they are so much farther away that they seem tiny.

The sun may be small for a star, but it is still much bigger than Earth. If the sun were the size of a skyscraper, Earth would be the size of a man. That's how huge the sun is when you compare it to the Earth. The moon, by the way, would be the size of a small dog standing next to the man.

The Earth is so small and so far away from the sun that it receives only one two-billionth part of the heat and light that the sun gives out. Yet this extremely narrow beam of light and heat rays make all the difference between a dark, dead world and the warm, beautiful Earth that we know.

The sun is a glowing ball of gases. It is said that the sun is at least 4,600,000,000 years old. Nobody really knows exactly how the sun was born in the first place, but one guess is that it was formed from a whirling mass of gases and dust. One of the reasons that some people want to explore space is to learn more about such wonders as how stars are born.

By studying other stars, people have made guesses about how long the sun will keep shining. At some time, the center of the sun will shrink and become hotter. The sun will then become a huge, red star, and the heat on Earth will get so high that life will not be able to exist. But don't worry. The people who study the sun tell us that this won't happen for at least another five billion years.

1 **About the Reading.** If the sentence is true according to the reading, write *true* on the line. If the sentence is not true according to the reading, write *false* on the line.

_____ 1. Both the sun and the moon are larger than the earth.

_____ 2. If it weren't for the sun, we wouldn't have any food.

_____ 3. Many people used to worship the sun.

_____ 4. People depend on plant life in order to live.

_____ 5. People do not really know how the sun was formed.

_____ 6. The sun gives off all its heat and light to the earth.

_____ 7. The sun is a glowing ball of liquids.

_____ 8. The sun is a star.

_____ 9. The sun is the largest star in our universe.

2 **Working with Headings.** Put the words below under the right heading.

air   oxygen
blood   rocks
carbon dioxide steam
chestnut trees steel
ice   water
orange juice   wine

Solids	**Liquids**	**Gases**
1. _____	1. _____	1. _____
2. _____	2. _____	2. _____
3. _____	3. _____	3. _____
4. _____	4. _____	4. _____

3 **Compound Words.** Match each word at the left with the sentence that best explains it.

cloudburst
moonlighting
moonshine
skylight
skyline
skyscraper
starfish
sunflower
sunstroke
suntan

_____

_____

_____

_____

_____

_____

_____

_____

_____

_____

1. This is a fish with five or more arms or rays which look like the points of a star.

2. This is a slang term for holding another job besides one's main job.

3. This is a slang term for whiskey that isn't lawful to make or sell.

4. This is a very tall building.

5. This is a window in a roof or a ceiling.

6. This is another word for a sudden rainstorm or downpour.

7. This is an outline of a city seen against the sky.

8. This is what happens to some people when they get too much sun.

9. This plant has a tall stem and large yellow flowers that have seeds which are rich in oil.

10. Many people go to the beach or lie in their backyards to get this.

4 **The Ending -ing.** Add -ing to the words listed below. Study the examples before you begin.

1. spell _Spelling_	1. please _pleasing_	1. begin _beginning_
2. cross _____	2. mine _____	2. jog _____
3. draw _____	3. merge _____	3. rig _____
4. color _____	4. bore _____	4. bid _____
5. coat _____	5. dare _____	5. top _____
6. belong _____	6. carve _____	6. mat _____

5 **Some Confusing -ing Words.** Fill in the blanks with the right answers.

1. staring *and* starring

   When Gail asked Rusty why he was _____ at the sign, he told her that he wanted

   to see who was _____ in the movie and, because he had forgotten his glasses, he was having trouble reading the names.

2. baring *and* barring

   When the manager heard that one of his players had been _____ his problems to

   the press, he made a rule _____ all reporters from the locker room.

3. griping *and* gripping

   As the man was _____ the pole in the subway car, he was _____ to anybody who would listen that the city ought to run more trains during rush hour.

4. hoping *and* hopping

   Mack was _____ to find a sales job in which he wouldn't be _____ from one city to the next so often.

5. filing *and* filling

   Anne was _____ in for the _____ clerk, who had left yesterday after work to visit his ailing mother.

Lesson 7

Thomas Edison

Edison National Historic Site

Words for Study

Thomas Edison	medicine	entire	baggage
results	Michigan	Port Huron	deaf
Ohio	overheard	conduct	deafness
Al	inspect	conductor	inventor
balloons	inspector	chemicals	inventions

Thomas Edison

Whenever you switch on a light bulb, play a record, or go to the movies, you are enjoying the results of things invented by a man named Thomas A. Edison. Edison was born in a small town in Ohio on February 11, 1847. As a small child, he was known for asking anybody he could find such questions as: How does a hen hatch chickens? What makes birds fly? Why does water put out fires?

Al—this is what his family called him—tried to find the answers to many of his questions himself. For example, once he collected some eggs and sat on them to see if they would hatch. Another time, after Al had learned that balloons fly because they are filled with gas, he talked a friend into taking a huge dose of medicine. Since Al knew this medicine caused a person to pass gas, he thought his friend would start flying any minute. Of course, all his friend did was lie ill on the ground while the whole world seemed to whirl around him.

When Al was seven years old, his family moved to Michigan. Al started school in Michigan and soon began to upset the teacher with all his questions. In this school, the teacher used a thick strap to whip young boys who asked too many questions.

One day, Al overheard the teacher tell the school inspector that the Edison boy was crazy. When Al told his mother this, she was so angry that she stormed into the teacher's classroom. She told him, "My son has more sense in his little finger than you have in your whole body!" She then took her son out of school and began to teach him herself. Thus, Thomas Edison only went to school for three months in his entire life!

At the age of twelve, Al got a job selling newspapers, candy, sandwiches, and peanuts on a train that ran between Port Huron and Detroit. In his spare time, he conducted tests with chemicals in the baggage car. One day, he had some bad luck. As a result, the baggage car caught on fire.

The conductor on the train, who was very angry, boxed Al's ears and threw him and all his things off the train. The conductor's blows may have caused Edison's later deafness, but Edison himself thought his deafness was because of something that happened to him later in life.

Edison never became completely deaf, although in his last years he could barely hear a shout. He didn't seem to mind, however, because he found that he could think much better if he couldn't hear what was going on around him.

Source material for this article: *World Book Encyclopedia.*

1 **About the Reading.** Answer these questions.

1. In what state was Thomas A. Edison born? _____

2. What is the date of his birth? _____

3. In what state did Edison go to school? _____

4. For how long did Edison go to school? _____

5. What was the nickname that Edison's family gave him? _____

6. For what reason did Edison talk his friend into taking some medicine?

_____

7. Why did Mrs. Edison take her son out of school?

_____

8. Why did a conductor throw Edison off the train?

_____

9. Why didn't Edison mind being almost completely deaf?

_____

10. List three things Edison invented.

   a. _____ b. _____ c. _____

11. Thomas A. Edison died on October 18, 1931. How old was he when he died? _____

What do you think?

12. It has been said that Thomas Edison wasn't much of a family man. Why do you think this was so?

_____

2 **More Work with Compound Words.** Thomas Edison is one well-known inventor. Through the ages, many people have invented things that have helped others. To find these inventions, read the clues listed below. Then choose a word from **List A** and add a word from **List B** to it. Match the invention with the sentence that best describes it. Study the example before you begin.

List A	List B
air	car
box	cuffs
dish	driver
gear	✓glass
hand	hammer
✓hour	lock
jack	maker
mouse	paper
pace	plane
pad	shift
sand	trap
screw	washer

hourglass   1. Before the invention of clocks, people used this to help them keep track of time.

_____   2. People use this invention to try to keep their homes and property safe from robbers.

_____   3. People who hate the sight of piles of dirty dishes love this invention.

_____   4. Police snap on this invention when they catch people they think have broken the law.

_____   5. This invention is a covered railway car that carries freight from one place to another.

_____   6. This invention is a hand tool used for turning screws.

_____   7. This invention is a machine used to drill rock.

_____   8. This invention is heavy paper coated on one side with sand and used for smoothing wood.

_____   9. This invention has been extremely helpful to people who have heart problems.

_____   10. This invention can be found in many automobiles.

_____   11. When two brothers successfully flew one of these for the first time in the early 1900's, they started a whole new way of getting from one place to another.

_____   12. All you need to make this invention work properly is a tiny bit of cheese and some starving mice.

3 **Which Word Fits Best?** Fill in each blank with the word that best completes the sentence.

1. Soap is to dirt as medicine is to _____.
   (a) disease   (b) doctor   (c) nurse   (d) pills

2. Entire is to whole as some is to _____.
   (a) everything   (b) nothing   (c) part   (d) total

3. Baggage is to suitcase as bag is to _____.
   (a) brown   (b) carry   (c) fill up   (d) knapsack

4. Baggage is to solid as gravy is to _____.
   (a) chemical   (b) gas   (c) liquid   (d) water

5. Blind is to eyes as deaf is to _____.
   (a) ears   (b) hearing   (c) noise   (d) sound

6. Program is to concert as menu is to _____.
   (a) diner   (b) dinner   (c) picnic   (d) sandwich

7. Detroit is to city as Michigan is to _____.
   (a) city   (b) country   (c) state   (d) town

8. Inspect is to study as gaze is to _____.
   (a) glance   (b) sight   (c) stare   (d) strain

9. Cause is to reason as effect is to _____.
   (a) problem   (b) reason   (c) result   (d) trouble

10. Conductor is to train as actor is to _____.
    (a) lines   (b) play   (c) role   (d) stage

4 **Syllables.** Each of the words listed below has either two or three syllables. Write these syllables on the lines to the right of each word.

1. receive   _____ • _____

2. skyline   _____ • _____

3. dishwasher   _____ • _____ • _____

4. worship   _____ • _____

5. railway   _____ • _____

6. beginning   _____ • _____ • _____

7. deafness   _____ • _____

8. compound   _____ • _____

9. jackhammer   _____ • _____ • _____

Lesson 8

Knives, Forks, and Spoons

Words for Study

caveman	item	soupspoon	cranberry
crudely	widely	Johnson	hamburgers
Italy	diagram	they've	apple
dining	American	turkey	ax
prongs	salad	berry	lying

Knives, Forks, and Spoons

The early caveman ate only enough food to stay alive. He did not think of eating as a nice way to pass the time, and he didn't care how sloppy he looked when he ate. The only eating tool he used was a spoon, which was very crudely made.

After thousands of years had passed, life was no longer so hard for people as it had been during the caveman's time. People started to think of eating as more than just something you had to do in order to stay alive. They began to care about how they looked while they were eating.

In 1100, the wife of a very rich man in Italy started to use forks at her dining room table because she thought people who picked up pieces of meat with their hands looked like animals. These early forks that she and others used had only two prongs. At first, not very many forks were made. It wasn't until four hundred years later that forks became a common item on the dining room tables in Italy.

The people in Italy also began to set their tables with knives at this time. Up until the 1500's, everyone carried a knife in his belt which was used at mealtime and any other time a knife was needed. When dinner was over, the guests would normally just wipe off their knives and stick them back into their belts. The knife and fork did not become widely used in France and England until the middle 1600's. The first fork was brought to America in 1630.

As people started to use knives, forks, and spoons all the time, they began to make up rules about how to set a table properly. For example, they decided that knives should always be to the right of the dinner plate with their cutting edges turned toward the plate. This rule doesn't sound as if it's too hard to learn, but if you were very rich and gave lots of fancy dinner parties, you would have to read books and study hard in order to know how to set a proper table.

Just to give you an idea of how complex setting a table can be, here is a diagram of a place setting for a fancy dinner party in America:

Key

1. Fish fork
2. Salad fork
3. Meat fork
4. Meat knife
5. Salad knife
6. Teaspoon
7. Soup spoon

Rubadeau/Kissinger

As you can see, eating has changed quite a bit since the caveman's time. If you are ever invited to a fancy dinner party, it might be a good idea to study up on all the different knives, forks, and spoons before you go. Or better yet, just watch what everybody else does before you begin to eat the food!

Copyright © 1973 by Reay Tannahill. Adapted from the book *Foods in History*. Reprinted with permission of Stein and Day Publishers.

1 **About the Reading.** Answer these questions.

1. Which came first—the knife, the fork, or the spoon? _____

2. In what country were forks first used? _____

3. Describe how people used a knife before the 1500's.

_____

4. What is the rule about where to place a knife when you set the table?

_____

5. Use the KEY to answer these questions about the diagram.

_____ a. What is the rounder spoon in this place setting used for?

_____ b. What is the fork closest to the plate used for?

_____ c. What is the knife closest to the plate used for?

_____ d. What is the number of the fork you would use if you were having a salad? (Write out the word.)

_____ e. What is the number of the fork you would use if you were having raw clams? (Write out the word.)

_____ f. For what reason would you use knife number five?

6. The reading is mainly about how _____

   (a) sloppy early caveman was when he ate.
   (b) people in Italy eat.
   (c) hard it is to set a table properly.
   (d) we came to use knives, forks, and spoons.

What do you think?

7. How would you like to eat a meal that had many knives and forks?

_____

2 **The Last Word on Knives.** Here is a verse from an American folk song in which another use for knives is given.

> The Johnson boys eat peas and honey.
> They've been eating this all their life.
> Makes the peas taste mighty funny,
> But it keeps them on the knife.

Do you think the Johnson boys would be invited to a fancy dinner party?
Be sure to explain your answer.

_____

_____

3 **Food for Thought.** Choose the best answer and write it on the line.

_____ 1. On which of these would you use a peeler?
(a) corn   (b) peas   (c) potatoes   (d) string beans

_____ 2. You cook spaghetti by _____ it.
(a) boiling   (b) broiling   (c) roasting   (d) toasting

_____ 3. For which of these do you _not_ need an oven?
(a) apple pie   (b) chocolate cake   (c) roast chicken   (d) stew

_____ 4. What would you need if you wanted to make doughnuts?
(a) deep frying pan   (b) oven   (c) saucepan   (d) toaster

_____ 5. If you were buying potatoes, you would buy them by the _____.
(a) gallon   (b) ounce   (c) pound   (d) quart

_____ 6. Which of these fruits can you eat without having to remove the seeds?
(a) berries   (b) oranges   (c) peaches   (d) prunes

_____ 7. What country comes to mind when you think of spaghetti?
(a) England   (b) Greece   (c) Italy   (d) Spain

_____ 8. With what do people normally stir their coffee?
(a) soupspoon   (b) tablespoon   (c) teaspoon   (d) finger

_____ 9. What kind of meal comes to mind when you think of ketchup?
(a) breakfast   (c) picnic
(b) New Year's Eve party   (d) Thanksgiving

_____ 10. What holiday makes you think of turkey and cranberry sauce?
(a) Easter   (c) New Year's Day
(b) Fourth of July   (d) Thanksgiving

4 **Singular and Plural Words.** Singular words have to do with just one of a thing. Plural words have to do with more than one of a thing. For example, _child_ is a singular word; _children_ is a plural word. State whether each word listed below is singular or plural. Study the examples before you begin.

1. ax   _singular_   7. items   _____

2. berries   _plural_   8. prayers   _____

3. cavemen   _____   9. result   _____

4. diagram   _____   10. salads   _____

5. hamburger _____   11. skyscraper _____

6. invention _____   12. turkey   _____

5 **One Knife/Two Knives.** Note how the singular form of *knife* is spelled with an *f*, and the plural form is spelled with a *v*. On the lines after the list of words at the left, write each word in its plural form. Then fill in the blanks of the sentences with the words from *both* lists. Study the examples before you begin.

✓ knife ✓ *knives* _____

life _____

shelf _____

leaf _____

loaf _____

half _____

1. George couldn't understand why he hadn't been invited

   because he had always thought of himself as the _____ of the party.

2. Herman bought a can of tomato soup, some Swiss cheese, and

   a small _____ of bread for his lunch.

3. It is said that cats have nine _____ .

4. Mary baked three _____ of oatmeal bread, and every single one of them was as hard as a rock.

5. Mrs. Carver owned only four *knives* _____ , so she decided to serve food that didn't need cutting at her dinner party.

6. Ms. Jones hid the Christmas presents on the top

   _____ in the cupboard.

7. The farmer split the piece of wood in _____ with his ax.

8. The _____ was so beautiful that Anne wished it could keep its color for a long, long time.

9. The _____ had to be raked before they rotted on the ground.

10. The police found a carving *knife* _____ lying next to the corpse.

11. The manager said that all the _____ had be cleaned before closing time.

12. Two _____ make a whole.

Lesson 9 ━━━━━━━━━━━━━━━━

Manners

Words for Study

manners	swallow	milkshake	bubbles
pockets	wind	release	swirl
pretend	bottom	squished	strawberry
tongue	dashboard	waitress	ill-mannered

Manners

While grownups are learning about knives, forks, and spoons, children are learning how to eat. "Don't talk with your mouth full. Don't gulp your food." These are just two of the many messages about manners that a child receives from grownups day in and day out.

Do children seem to enjoy learning about manners? I don't think so. In this lesson, you will read what one writer has to say about children's ideas of manners in a funny story called "How to Eat Like a Child."

Peas. Mash into thin sheet on plate. Press back of fork into peas. Hold fork with the prongs pointed straight up and lick off peas.

Sandwiches. Leave the crusts. If your mother says you have to eat them because it's the best part, stuff them into your pockets or between the seats of the couch.

French fries. Wave one French fry in the air while you talk. Pretend that you're leading a band. Place four French fries in mouth at once and chew. Turn to your sister and stick out tongue coated with French fries. Close mouth and swallow. Smile.

Spaghetti. Wind too many strands on fork and make sure at least two strands are hanging down. Open mouth wide and stuff in spaghetti. Make as much noise as you can as you suck in hanging strands. Clean plate, ask for seconds, and eat only half. When carrying plate to kitchen, hold tilted so that remaining spaghetti slides onto floor.

Ice cream. Ask for double scoop. Knock the top scoop off while walking out the door. Cry. Lick remaining scoop slowly so that ice cream melts down outside of the cone and over your hand. Stop licking when ice cream is even with top of cone. Eat a hole in the bottom of the cone and suck the rest of the ice cream out the bottom. When only the cone remains with ice cream coating the inside, leave on car dashboard.

Milkshake. Bite off one end of paper that covers straw. Blow through straw to shoot paper across table. Place straw in milkshake and suck. When liquid just reaches your mouth, place a finger over top of straw. Lift straw out of shake, put bottom end in mouth, release finger and swallow.

Do this until straw is squished so you can't suck through it. Ask for another. This time, shoot paper at the waitress when she isn't looking. Sip your milkshake slowly as if you are just minding your own business. When there is about an inch of liquid remaining, blow through straw until bubbles rise to top of glass. When your mom or dad says he's had just about enough, say you're sick.

Adapted and reprinted with permission from *How to Eat Like a Child* by Delia Ephron. Published by Viking Press. Copyright © 1979 by Delia Ephron.

1 What Do You Think?

1. Why do you think most children believe learning about manners is either awful or boring?

_____

2. Describe how you ate something as a child which made either your mother or father really angry.

_____

_____

_____

3. How do you react when you see an ill-mannered child or grownup?

_____

2 **Which Word Does Not Fit?** Choose the word from each group that does not fit with the rest and write it on the line to the right. Study the example before you begin.

1. chocolate   *ice cream* \
    fudge swirl \
√ ice cream \
    strawberry \
    vanilla

7. chew \
   food \
   gulp \
   sip \
   swallow

2. manners \
   menu \
   order \
   tip \
   waitress

8. billionth \
   entire \
   everything \
   total \
   whole

3. crude \
   ill-mannered \
   release \
   rough \
   rude

9. automobile \
   brake \
   dashboard \
   floorboard \
   steering wheel

4. cook \
   dinner \
   manager \
   waiter \
   waitress

10. crowbar \
    jackhammer \
    pacemaker \
    screwdriver \
    wrench

5. apple \
   beet \
   cranberry \
   lime \
   pear

11. Huron \
    Michigan \
    New York \
    Ohio \
    Washington

6. jeans \
   pants \
   pockets \
   slacks \
   trousers

12. cheek \
    chin \
    feet \
    nose \
    tongue

3 **Recipes.** Put the steps of these recipes in the right order on the lines below each recipe.

Fried Chicken

Brown chicken slowly until skin is crisp and golden.
Put flour, salt, pepper and chicken in paper bag.
Drain on paper towels.
Shake until chicken is well coated.
Melt butter or fat in deep frying pan.

1. _____
2. _____
3. _____
4. _____
5. _____

Green Salad

Just before serving, pour ¼ cup dressing over greens.
Tear into bite-size pieces.
Wash greens and throw away any stems.
Toss lightly until dressing coats leaves.
Chill greens in bowl until serving time.

1. _____
2. _____
3. _____
4. _____
5. _____

4 **Singular and Plural Words.** Put the singular words in the list at the left under the heading marked **Singular**. Put the plural words under the heading marked **Plural**.

	Singular	Plural
batteries	1. ———————	1. ———————
bubble	2. ———————	2. ———————
channel	3. ———————	3. ———————
children	4. ———————	4. ———————
concept	5. ———————	5. ———————
desert	6. ———————	6. ———————
effect	7. ———————	7. ———————
heroes	8. ———————	8. ———————
league	9. ———————	9. ———————
meadow	10. ———————	10. ———————

batteries
bubble
channel
children
concept
desert
effect
heroes
league
meadow
menu
message
museums
pocket
spiders
strawberries
tongues
waitresses
women
Yankees

5 **More about Manners.** People have written a lot about manners. See if you know what the experts have to say about these matters. Put the letter you think matches their ideas on the line to the left.

———— 1. When you shake someone's hand, ————
(a) you should keep your gloves on if you are wearing gloves.
(b) you should extend your hand first if you are a woman.
(c) you should wait until the woman extends her hand if you are a man.
(d) your grip should be firm.

———— 2. When a lady's maid is working, her dress should be ————
(a) black.
(b) brown.
(c) gray.
(d) white.

3. At a fancy dinner party, what kind of wine should you serve with fish?

    (a) a dry red wine
    (b) a dry white wine
    (c) a sweet red wine
    (d) a sweet white wine

4. At a very large party, how many dressing rooms should you have for your guests?

    (a) none
    (b) one
    (c) two
    (d) three

5. When you hire a nurse to look after your children, you should always _____

    (a) find out how much she knows about medicine.
    (b) let your children do the hiring.
    (c) put an ad in the newspaper.
    (d) talk to the people she worked for in the past.

6. When "The Star-Spangled Banner" is played, you should _____

    (a) keep your voice down if you are talking to a friend.
    (b) rise at once and stand with respect.
    (c) sing only if you can reach the high notes.
    (d) stand only if you are an American.

7. When you get a message that someone has phoned you while you were out, you should _____

    (a) decide whether or not the call is really important.
    (b) return the call as soon as you can.
    (c) return the call only if you really feel like it.
    (d) try to see the person who called you at once.

8. If you are watching TV and guests drop by to see you, you should _____

    (a) change the channel to a program they want to see.
    (b) offer them a drink.
    (c) tell them to come back when the program is over.
    (d) turn off the TV set.

9. Who normally pays the cost of a wedding?

    (a) the bride
    (b) the groom
    (c) the mother and father of the bride
    (d) the mother and father of the groom

10. What do you think of all these rules about how people should act?

    (a) They're silly.
    (b) They're important.
    (c) Some of them are important.
    (d) It doesn't matter how you act.

Lesson 10

Flying Saucers

Flying saucers in the movie *War of the Worlds*

Words for Study

A.M.	immense	hailstones	belief
upward	reflected	connected	planet
disc	meteor	continue	view
movement	meteorite	Santa Claus	atmosphere

Flying Saucers

On January 7, 1954, at 4:26 A.M., a baker in a French town decided to step outside for a breath of fresh air. A strange glow in the sky made him look upward. What he saw was a shining disc hanging in the sky. The disc was as big as a full moon but much brighter.

The baker could not believe his eyes, but the object was surely there and not very far above the town either. It remained for many seconds and started a rocking movement. Then the strange object discharged a flash of light which lit up the whole town square. At last, it took off at an immense speed toward the coast. The entire sky seemed filled with a huge, orange-colored light.

This is just one of many reports given by people who have seen flying saucers. As far as anyone knows, the term "flying saucer" was invented by an American in 1947. This American had also seen something very strange in the sky while he was flying an airplane above the state of Washington. Only instead of seeing just one object, as the French baker had, the American saw nine of these gleaming discs moving through space at about a thousand miles per hour. Since they were shaped like pie pans, the American decided to call them "flying saucers."

Flying saucer in the movie *The Day the Earth Stood Still*

Collectors Book Store

Flying saucer in the movie *Close Encounters of the Third Kind*

In the United States, most of the people who have been hired to find out whether or not flying saucers really exist think that there is no such thing. They claim that those who say they have seen a flying saucer have either seen something else or are just plain crazy. One idea is that a flying saucer is nothing more than reflected light from the sun on a low-hanging cloud. Another idea is that what the flying saucer "nuts" are really seeing are weather balloons, small meteors, or large hailstones.

There is still a group, which is connected with an Air Force base in Ohio, that checks out reports of flying saucers. However, most Americans, as well as people in other countries, continue to think that flying saucers are about as real as Santa Claus.

One reason for the strong belief that flying saucers are not real is that most of us believe life exists only on the planet Earth. It is a well-known fact that there are at least 40 billion suns besides our own sun. Then why is it that people can't picture life in other places?

One man answers this question by saying that people on Earth have "a fish's eye view" of everything. What he means is that a trout, for example, who can see only water above him, thinks that nothing can live out of water. And this is exactly the concept we people on Earth have: we can't picture life in any other place except the one we know.

Adapted and reprinted by permission of S.G. Phillips, Inc. from *The Truth About Flying Saucers* by Aime Michel. Copyright © 1956 by S.G. Phillips, Inc.

1 **About the Reading.** Answer these questions.

1. List two places named in this reading where flying saucers have been sighted.

   _____ and _____

2. In what year was the term "flying saucer" first used? _____

3. Explain the difference between what the first man in France saw and the second man in Washington saw.

   _____

   _____

4. What three objects do some people claim flying saucers really are?

   a. _____ b. _____ c. _____

5. What group in the United States still studies flying saucers?

   _____

6. Why is it so hard to believe in flying saucers according to the man who stated the "fish's eye view"?

   _____

   _____

What do you think?

7. Do you think that more people believe in flying saucers now than in earlier times? (Be sure to explain your answer.)

   _____

   _____

8. How would you react if you met someone or something from outer space?

   _____

2 **More about Meteors.** Use the words at the left to fill in the blanks so the sentences make sense. Take your time!

because
collected
entering
explode
heard
hot
outside
piece
shine
space
stars
200,000,000

A meteor is a _____ of stony matter that comes into Earth's atmosphere from _____. Meteors cannot be seen until they enter the atmosphere. Then, they become so _____ that they glow, and we can see them _____ .

Meteors are often called shooting stars or falling stars _____ they look like _____ falling from the sky.

It is said that as many as _____ meteors can be seen _____ Earth's atmosphere every day. Meteors that reach Earth before burning up are called meteorites. These meteorites sometimes _____ with a noise that can be _____ for miles when they strike Earth or its atmosphere.

Meteorites are _____ for study because they come from _____ Earth.

3 **Choosing the Right Word.** Choose the word in the line that describes, is an example of, or means the same thing as the first word and write it on the line to the right.

1. **flying saucer:**	circle	disc	square	airplane	_____
2. **a.m.:**	dusk	noon	evening	morning	_____
3. **meteor:**	icy	phony	stony	scratchy	_____
4. **star:**	Earth	sun	meteor	meteorite	_____
5. **connected:**	related	removed	renewed	repaired	_____
6. **planet:**	Earth	sun	meteor	meteorite	_____
7. **downpour:**	hail	cloudy	hailstone	cloudburst	_____
8. **idea:**	concept	excuse	reason	thinking	_____
9. **disc:**	prong	record	balloon	hailstone	_____
10. **invention:**	sunburn	sundown	sunrise	sunglasses	_____

4 **Word Study.** Each of the six words at the left has two meanings. A few of these words can be said two ways even though they are spelled the same way. Use each word *twice* in the twelve sentences below.

lying
racket
tears
use
wind
wound

1. Bobby's little sister was making such a _____ that he wasn't able to keep his mind on his homework.

2. "It's no _____," shouted the policemen to the robbers. "Come on out with your hands up."

3. Are you aware that if you _____ your watch too tightly, it will no longer work?

4. Ms. Baker _____ her watch so tightly that it stopped working.

5. When Mary finds a mistake in her work, she always _____ up her paper and starts all over again.

6. Paul asked Sue if he could borrow her tennis _____ for the weekend.

7. Some men think that women _____ tears in order to get what they want.

8. The doctor told Thomas that he would have to have stitches because the _____ was so deep.

9. The police were informed that a body was _____ in front of a brick building between Fourth and Main Streets.

10. The _____ was so strong that people had to hold onto their hats.

11. When George Washington's father told his son he thought he was _____, George replied, "Father, I cannot tell a lie."

12. _____ of joy streamed down the father's face when he was informed that his son was safe.

Review: Lessons 1-10

1 **Answer These Questions.** Fill in the blanks with the right answers.

_____ 1. Is the sun a meteor, a planet, or a star?

_____ 2. Is the sun made up of gases, liquids, or solids?

_____ 3. Is a flying saucer a circle, a disc, or a square?

_____ 4. Does a meteorite burn up, reach the Earth, or stay in space?

_____ 5. Did Thomas A. Edison invent the automobile, the light bulb, or the subway?

_____ 6. Did Edison become blind, deaf, or dumb in his later years?

_____ 7. According to Lesson 8, was the first fork used in Egypt, France, or Italy?

_____ 8. Is mincemeat pie a common dessert at Easter, Thanksgiving, or the Fourth of July?

2 **Word Study.** Choose the right answer and write it on the line.

_____ 1. Prayer is a form of _____.
(a) business   (b) church   (c) Sunday   (d) worship

_____ 2. A diagram is a _____.
(a) drawing   (b) feeling   (c) idea   (d) story

_____ 3. An ill-mannered person acts _____.
(a) crudely   (b) fussy   (c) high-class   (d) widely

_____ 4. Who would you expect to find in a lab?
(a) actor   (b) conductor   (c) inspector   (d) inventor

_____ 5. If you are given a dose of something, it is normally _____.
(a) chemicals   (b) medicine   (c) milkshake   (d) whiskey

_____ 6. Prongs are a part of a _____.
(a) fork   (b) knife   (c) soupspoon   (d) spoon

_____ 7. The city Rome is in _____.
(a) Asia   (b) Italy   (c) Spain   (d) the United States

_____ 8. If a doctor wants to look at your throat, he commands you
to stick out your _____.
(a) finger   (b) lips   (c) throat   (d) tongue

_____ 9. A swirling movement is _____.
(a) back and forth   (b) up and down   (c) upward   (d) whirling

_____ 10. An example of a disc is a(n) _____.
(a) atmosphere   (b) hailstone   (c) planet   (d) record

3 **Words That Mean the Same.** Match each word at the left with the word that has
the same meaning.

beam	_____ 1. come in
connected	
continue	_____ 2. eating
dining	_____ 3. go on
enter	
entire	_____ 4. joined
pretend	_____ 5. let go
release	
sloppy	_____ 6. make-believe
sudden	_____ 7. messy
swirl	
tale	_____ 8. quick
	_____ 9. ray
	_____ 10. story
	_____ 11. whirl
	_____ 12. whole

4 Word Opposites. Match each word at the left with the word that means nearly the opposite.

believe in
bottom
daring
downward
immense
lying
narrow
release
skyscraper
sloppy
swallow
worried

_____ 1. calm

_____ 2. "chicken"

_____ 3. hold on

_____ 4. hut

_____ 5. mistrust

_____ 6. neat

_____ 7. spit out

_____ 8. tiny

_____ 9. top

_____ 10. truthful

_____ 11. upward

_____ 12. wide

5 Syllables.
In the box below are some syllables that you can use to make words. The words will fit into the ten sentences. No syllable is used twice and no syllables should be left over when you are done. The number after each sentence tells you how many syllables are in each word. Study the example before you begin.

A	at	ber	ber	ca	cave	cine	cran	~~et~~	gan
Hu	i	i	i	med	men	mer	Mich	mos	phere
~~pock~~	ress	ron	ry	ry	straw	wait			

pocket   1. This is where most men keep their wallets. (2)

_____ 2. She takes your order and hands you the check. (2)

_____ 3. Detroit is one of the cities in this state. (3)

_____ 4. A drug used to treat disease is called _____ . (3)

_____ 5. This is another word for the United States. (4)

_____ 6. This is what they called people who lived during the Stone Age. (2)

_____ 7. This kind of sauce is often served at a Thanksgiving meal. (3)

_____ 8. This red fruit is used to make shortcake. (3)

_____ 9. This is what the gases around the Earth are called. (3)

_____ 10. This is the name of one of the five Great Lakes in the United States. (2)

6 **Menus.** Write the names of the foods below under the proper headings.

apple pie   ketchup   potato salad
corn flakes   oatmeal   sweet potatoes
cranberry sauce   orange juice   toast
dressing   pickles   turkey
hamburgers   poached eggs   ants

Breakfast	**Thanksgiving Dinner**	**Picnic**
1. _____	1. _____	1. _____
2. _____	2. _____	2. _____
3. _____	3. _____	3. _____
4. _____	4. _____	4. _____
5. _____	5. _____	5. _____

7 **The Sound for -le.** Use the words at the left to fill in the blanks.

able
apples
Bible
bubble
double
gentle
gobble
little
middle
single
struggle
table

Once upon a time, there was a _____ old woman who lived in a small

apartment in the _____ of a huge city. Because she was so old, she was no

longer _____ to work. All the neighbors were very _____ with her.

They would bring her such treats as beautiful red _____ and sweet pink

_____ gum. The apples were nice, but it was the gum she loved most. She

would _____ up each piece and blow huge bubbles as she sat in her

rocking chair reading verses from the _____ day after day.

One Thursday afternoon, a robber sneaked into the lady's apartment. He
took one look at the lady and thought to himself, "Well, this one can't put up

much of a _____."

The robber was sadly mistaken. As he was sneaking toward her, the lady was

just blowing the biggest bubble in the world. In fact, it was not a _____

bubble; it was a _____ bubble. Pop! Pop! The two bubbles burst all
over the robber's face and body.

When the police got there twenty minutes later, they found the robber hiding

under the kitchen _____. He was still trying to get the bubble gum off his
face and clothing. After all, how could he go back out on the streets looking like
such a jerk!

Word Index: Lessons 1-10

A
action
affect
airplane
Al
A.M.
America
American
amount
anyone
apple
artery
Asia
atmosphere
aware
ax(e)

B
Babe
baggage
baggy
balloon
Baltimore
Bambino
battery
beam
beginning
belief
believer
belly
belonging
berry
bidder
bidding
billionth
blender
blindness
boring
borrow
bottom
boxcar
boxing
brandy
breadboard
breather
breezy
broiler
bubble
built
bully
bunny
bushy
butterfly
buzzer

C
carbon
carbon dioxide
Carver, G.W.

carving
caveman
channel
chat
chemical
choosy
choppy
Christmas Eve
clammy
cloudburst
coating
collect
color
coloring
concept
conduct
conductor
connect
continue
cooky
cranberry
creamy
crisp
crossing
crudely
curly

D
daring
dashboard
deaf
deafness
dealer
degree
desert
diagram
dial
digger
dining
disc
disease
dishwasher
downward
drawing
drummer
dusty

E
Edison, T.
effect
entire
exhale

F
fatty
feeler
flicker
flipper
floorboard
floppy

flowery
forest

G
gearshift
god
grasshopper
gravy
greasy
gummy
gunner

H
hailstone
half-hour
hamburger
handcuff
hearing
Herman
hero
hiker
holiday
hot dog
Huron

I
ill-mannered
immense
inch
Indian
insider
inspect
inspector
intermission
invader
invention
inventor
Italy
item

J
jackhammer
jog
jogger
jogging
Johnson
jumper

K
killer

L
ladybug
latch
leafy
league
learner
lightly
likely
liner
locate
locker

logger
lying

M
make-believe
manners
matting
meadow
medicine
menu
merging
message
meteor
meteorite
Michigan
milkshake
mining
moody
moonlight
moonshine
mound
mousetrap
mousy
mouthpart
movement
muggy
museum

N
narrow
nervy
nevertheless
normal
normally

O
object
offer
Ohio
one-fourth
one-third
orange
outline
outsider
overheard
oxygen

P
pacemaker
paddle
padlock
panty
pasty
patter
peppy
per
perform
performer
picnic
planet
pleasing

plural
pocket
pollen
polo
potty
prayer
pretend
printer
process
program
prompt
prong
Pueblo

Q

R
racket
railway
rainstorm
ray
reader
reading
receive
reflect
release
result
rigging
runner
rusty

S
salad
sandpaper
sandy
Santa Claus
scaly
scary
screwdriver
setting
shaker
shortcut
silky
singular
skipper
skylight
skyline
skyscraper
slop
sloppy
smoggy
snapper
soapy
soupspoon
Southwest
sox
speedy
spelling
spider
spongy

squish
stadium
starfish
steal
steer
stomp
strainer
strawberry
string bean
stroll
sudden
sunflower
sunstroke
suntan
swallow
swamp
swirl

T
tennis
termite
they've
Thomas
tiny
toe
Tommy
tongue
topping
total
trader
training
tuner
turkey
TV

U
unaware
upper
upward
used

V
vein
view

W
waitress
washer
watcher
wheezy
whiskey
widely
wind
wiper
worry
worship

X

Y
Yankee
yellow

Z

Lesson 11

Accepting Who You Are

Words for Study

friendship	statements	M.D.	loneliness
accepting	truly	battleship	agreement
high-priced	fever	basement	disagreement
therefore	growth	laziness	innings

Accepting Who You Are

How you see yourself and how you feel about yourself are very important for many reasons. How you feel about yourself shows in everything you do or choose not to do. You show how you feel about yourself in the way you walk and talk, the way you laugh and cry, the way you dress and have fun, the way you get angry and find happiness.

Other people do not normally sit down and make lists of all the things they like and don't like about you. Who has time to do this? Nevertheless, you do impress others. If you impress others as being an angry or unhappy person, they won't want to be around you for very long. If you impress others as being a friendly and open person, the chances are that others will want your friendship.

This does not mean that you have to act in a certain way in order to be liked. Nobody likes a phony—except, maybe, another phony. What you have to do is work at really accepting yourself because as you learn to accept yourself, you will become more open and friendly. Only people who feel bad about themselves have to pretend to be friendly and open.

The person who has learned to accept himself normally stands in a relaxed way. He does not have to force his slouched shoulders back because he doesn't have slouched shoulders. The person who has learned to accept himself normally dresses in clothes that he can afford to buy and take care of. He does not feel he has to spend all his wages on fancy clothes because he has so much to offer others that he (or she) does not need a high-priced suit or dress in order to feel good. The person who has learned to accept himself does not get angry every time he doesn't get what he wants. Because he accepts himself, he doesn't demand that everybody else treat him like a king. He doesn't think everybody else is out to get him either. The person who accepts himself can accept other people. Therefore, this person does not often feel really angry or upset.

What does it mean to accept yourself? You have often heard people say, "Okay, I admit I'm that way, but that's just the way I am." People who make statements like this often think they are accepting themselves as they are, but they're just kidding themselves. When you really accept yourself, you don't judge yourself. Also, you don't give up. The person who truly accepts himself says something like this: "I am I, and whatever I am, I accept me as me. Now, how can I take what I am and use what I am so I can have good health, good friendships, and greater happiness?" The person who can truly accept himself lives each minute of his day with hope in his heart and the strong belief in his mind that his life will continue to change for the better.

Do not think that changing for the better is a straight, painless line. Learning to accept ourselves and changing for the better are like a fever curve—there are ups and downs. We take five steps forward, two steps back, five more steps forward, etc. There are bumps in the road, but these are only growing pains. In real growth, these growing pains always lead to a real change for the better.

Adapted from *The Winner's Notebook* by Theodore Isaac Rubin, M.D.
Used with permission of the author.

1 **About the Reading.** Answer these questions.

1. True or false? Write *true* on the line if the statement agrees with what you just read. Write *false* on the line if the statement disagrees with what you just read.

_____ a. A person who says, "Well, that's just the way I am" accepts himself.

_____ b. Most people really don't care if others act in a phony way.

_____ c. How you feel about yourself shows in everything you do.

_____ d. Other people keep close track of what they like and don't like about you.

_____ e. People who accept themselves are open and friendly.

_____ f. Changing your ways is fairly easy.

_____ g. People who accept themselves judge themselves.

_____ h. People who don't accept themselves are treated like kings.

_____ i. All people think life is pretty hopeless.

_____ j. When people are changing, they get fevers.

What do you think?

2. Describe a change you have made in yourself that has made your life happier for you.

_____

_____

_____

3. Do you agree or disagree with what this writer has to say about accepting yourself? Be sure to explain your answer.

_____

_____

_____

2 **Changing the y to i.** Study the example before you begin. Say the words out loud after you have written them.

1. happy   _happier_   _happiest_   _happiness_

2. lazy   _____   _____   _____

3. lonely   _____   _____   _____

4. easy   _____   _____   _____

5. moody   _____   _____   _____

6. busy   _____   _____   _____

3 **Word Endings.** Use the words in each group at the left to fill in the blanks.

Words that end with *-ship.*

battleship
friendship
worship

1. Even though Bob knew it might end their _____, he decided to tell Andy that he had bad breath.

2. Some men and women want the people they are in love with to _____ the ground they walk on.

3. The _____ was turned into a hotel after the war ended.

Words that end with *-ment.*

agreement
apartment
basement
disagreement
statement

1. Because of their _____ with the boss, the workers in the shop decided to strike.

2. In many houses, the fuse box is located in the _____.

3. Mack made an _____ to paint the house in return for free room and board.

4. The judge said, "Strike that last _____ from the record."

5. When the landlord raised the rent, Kit decided to look for another

_____.

Words that end with *-ness.*

blindness
business
deafness
happiness
laziness
loneliness

1. Being around loud noises all the time can cause _____.

2. In spite of the _____ she felt, Joyce refused to go out and meet people because she thought people should come to her.

3. On Friday morning, Scott was fired from his job because of his

_____.

4. The doctor told Mr. and Mrs. Martin that their daughter's

_____ could be cured.

5. Many people believe that having more money will bring them greater _____.

6. Whenever Mr. Jones asked his wife where she had spent the afternoon, she would turn around and snap at him, "Mind your own _____!"

4 **Silent Letters.** Write each word on the line to the right and draw a line through the silent letter. Study the example before you begin.

1. gnat   ~~g~~nat

6. thumb _____

2. kneel _____

7. wrist _____

3. wrench _____

8. lamb _____

4. dumb _____

9. wren _____

5. wrap _____

10. numb _____

5 Happiness. Can you figure out this quote about happiness?

A. Each of the ten sentences describes a certain word. Write that word on the lines to the left of each sentence.

B. Put the letters of these words in the blanks at the bottom of the page. The quote, when all the blanks are filled in, will be about happiness.

C. The first sentence has been done for you. Study it before you begin.

B A R B E R S
11 36 4 11 41 26 28

1. These people shave other people and cut hair for a living.

___ ___ T ___ ___
29 9 20 − 30 26

2. On this holiday, many children hunt for eggs and baskets.

___ ___ ___ T ___ ___ ___
1 16 34 6 − 23 12 19

3. Nine plus nine is _____.

___ ___ ___ ___ ___ L
8 36 27 27 36 −

4. The whale is not a fish; it's a _____.

___ ___ ___ ___ ___ ___
31 40 18 2 3 42

5. The plural of knife is _____.

___ ___ ___ ___ ___ ___ ___
24 1 11 26 7 36 26 5

6. The second month of the year is _____.

___ ___ ___ ___ ___
35 9 37 38 5

7. People do not want to be sad; they want to be _____.

___ ___ ___ ___
22 21 25 10

8. Do you know the song which contains the line, "I've got the sun in the morning and the _____ at night"?

___ ___ ___ ___
43 39 15 19

9. The salesman told Sam that all he had to do was _____ his name on the dotted line.

___ ___ ___ ___ ___ ___ ___
32 33 10 13 14 15 17

10. In a baseball game, there are nine _____ unless the score is tied.

Quote: ___ ___ ___ R ___ ___   ___ ___ ___ ___ ___   B ___ ___ ___ ___   ___ ___
1 2 3 4 5   6 7 8 9 10   11 12 13 14 15   16 17

___ ___   ___ ___ ___ ___   ___ ___ R ___   S ___ ___ ___ ___ ___ ___
18 19   20 21 22 23   24 25 26 27   28 29 30 31 32 33 34

___ A ___ ___ ___ ___ E ___ ___.
35 36 37 38 39 40 41 42 43

Lesson 12

Anne Frank: Part I

The Bettmann Archive

Words for Study

Frank	Amsterdam	diary	shred
German	Holland	North Pole	cattle
office	Jewish	heaps	escape
officer	Adolf Hitler	depressing	radio
attic	World War II	dozen	perhaps

Anne Frank: Part I

In August, 1944, a German soldier and four police broke into a small attic in the city of Amsterdam, which is in the country Holland. They found eight people who had been living there in hiding for twenty-five months. These people had been in hiding because they were Jewish.

Adolf Hitler was the German ruler at the time, and his army had taken control of Holland and many other countries. Hitler had vowed to get rid of all Jews. By the end of World War II in 1945, six million Jews would be dead because of Hitler's belief that all Jews should be killed.

Anne Frank, a young Jewish girl, was one of the eight people living in the attic. Later, she died in one of the many camps which Hitler had built in order to get rid of the Jews. However, what the German officer did not find when his men raided the attic in Amsterdam was a small diary that Anne had kept during the time her family and four other people lived there.

This diary is widely read and loved to this day. The diary not only describes life in the cramped attic, but also is proof that some people are able to hold onto their faith in spite of the pain that life can often bring.

Anne Frank called her diary "Kitty." Here are some of the thoughts and feelings that she wrote to "Kitty" between the ages of thirteen and fifteen as she lived in the attic:

Wednesday, 8 July, 1942
Dear Kitty,

Mommy called me at 5:30 the next morning. We put on heaps of clothes as if we were going to the North Pole, the only reason being to take clothes with us. No Jew would have dreamed of going out with a suitcase full of clothing. . . .

The hiding place itself would be in the building where Daddy had his office. The first day we were there, we unpacked boxes, filled cupboards, hammered, and straightened our new home up until we were dead beat. We hadn't had a bit of anything warm the whole day, but we didn't care. Mommy and my sister were too tired and keyed up, and Daddy and I were too busy.

Friday, 9 October, 1942
Dear Kitty,

I've only got depressing news today. Our many Jewish friends are being taken away by the dozen. These people are being treated by the German police without a shred of respect. They are loaded into cattle trucks and sent to a big Jewish camp where there is only one place to wash for a hundred people and not nearly enough bathrooms. Men, women, and children all sleep together. A lot of the women, and even girls, who stay there for any amount of time are expecting babies.

There is no escape from these camps. Most of the people are branded as inmates by their shaved heads and also by their Jewish looks. We think that most of them are murdered. The English radio tells us that they are being gassed. Perhaps that is the quickest way to die.

Nice people, the Germans! To think that I was once one of them, too! No, Hitler took away our country long ago.

Continued in the next lesson . . .

1 About the Reading. Answer these questions.

1. Amsterdam is a city in the country of _____ .

2. The Frank family lived in hiding for _____ months before they were found by the German police.

3. The ruler of Germany during this time was _____ .

4. What had this ruler vowed to do? _____

5. What fact tells you that the German ruler tried to keep this vow?

   _____

6. What is the name of the war that is taking place during this time? _____

7. Explain why Anne's family wore so many clothes when they escaped to this hiding place.

   _____

8. Describe the kind of place in which the Frank family hid from the Germans.

   _____

9. List four statements that Anne Frank makes which describe how the Jewish people were treated "without a shred of respect" by the Germans.

   a. _____

   b. _____

   c. _____

   d. _____

10. What is one way that Anne and her family heard about what was going on in the outside world?

    _____

What do you think?

11. Why do you think Anne Frank gives her diary a name?

    _____

12. How do you think you would have acted if you had been living during this time?

    _____

    _____

2 **Word Beginnings.** Choose the word which *best* completes each sentence and write it on the line.

1. Anne Frank enjoyed reading so much that she might have been called a

   _____ by her friends.
   (a) bookcase   (b) bookshelf   (c) bookstore   (d) bookworm

2. Adolf Hitler was _____ to the belief that Jewish people should be killed.
   (a) comforted   (b) committed   (c) concerned   (d) confronted

3. Because of Hitler's actions, many Jews found themselves _____.
   (a) homebodies   (b) homeless   (c) homemade   (d) homesick

4. Many Germans, besides the Jews, were treated by Hitler's men as if they were _____.
   (a) catbirds   (b) catcalls   (c) catfish   (d) cattle

5. At first, many leaders of the other countries did not see just how bad Hitler was.

   They _____ him completely.
   (a) miscounted   (b) misjudged   (c) misplaced   (d) mistreated

6. Hitler gained so much control that it became more and more _____
   that the German people would be able to rise up against him.
   (a) unafraid   (b) unless   (c) unlikely   (d) unlucky

7. _____, people began to fear this ruler who had said he would
   bring peace and happiness to the German people.
   (a) Everybody   (b) Everyone   (c) Everything   (d) Everywhere

8. Hitler's dream of ruling the world _____ on him.
   (a) backbone   (b) backfired   (c) backpacked   (d) backtracked

9. After Hitler's _____, thousands of people had to pick up the
   pieces of their lives and start all over again.
   (a) downfall   (b) downhill   (c) downright   (d) downtown

10. Museums have been built to honor those who died during World War II and also

    to _____ us how much we must work to guard our freedom.
    (a) rejoice   (b) remain   (c) remind   (d) respond

11. It is sad that, for so many people, their _____ of freedom is just getting
    what they want when they want it.
    (a) concern   (b) concept   (c) consent   (d) content

12. However, when you stop to think about it, this kind of thinking often means

    ending up as a _____ for someone else's schemes—just as many
    Germans did during Hitler's rule.
    (a) doorbell   (b) doorknob   (c) doormat   (d) doorway

3 **Words That Mean the Same.** Match each word at the left with the word that has nearly the same meaning.

basement

depressed

dozen

excite

inflate

inmate

M.D.

perhaps

slaughter

truly

_____ 1. cellar

_____ 2. convict

_____ 3. doctor

_____ 4. expand

_____ 5. kill

_____ 6. maybe

_____ 7. really

_____ 8. thrill

_____ 9. twelve

_____ 10. unhappy

4 **Word Opposites.** Match each word at the left with the word that means nearly the opposite.

accept

attic

blindness

cheap

depressed

disagreement

fever

glance

North Pole

outskirts

_____ 1. agreement

_____ 2. basement

_____ 3. chills

_____ 4. downtown

_____ 5. high-priced

_____ 6. joyful

_____ 7. refuse

_____ 8. sight

_____ 9. South Pole

_____ 10. stare

5 **Words That End in Hard or Soft** *g.* Put the words in the list under the proper headings. Study the example before you begin.

	Soft *g*	Hard *g*
badge	*badge*	*beg*
beg		
binge		
brag		
egg		
garbage		
gorge		
jog		
misjudge		
shrug		
verge		
underdog		

Lesson 13

Words for Study

mustn't	Peter	thunder	Poland
kindness	freely	heavens	Japan
kindhearted	ideals	terrible	Germany
selfish	foolish	history	Pearl Harbor
nature	wilderness	attacked	Hawaii

Anne Frank: Part II

Saturday, 30 January, 1943
Dear Kitty,

I'm boiling with rage, and yet I mustn't show it. I'd like to stamp my feet, scream, give Mommy a good shaking, cry, and I don't know what else because of the awful words and mocking looks which are sent my way every day.

I would like to shout to all of them—"Leave me in peace. Let me sleep one night at least without my pillow being wet with tears, my eyes burning, and my head throbbing. Let me get away from it all!"

But I can't do that. I can't let them see the wounds which they have caused. I couldn't bear their kindness and kindhearted jokes. It would only make me scream all the more. If I talk, everyone thinks I'm showing off; when I don't talk, they think I'm silly. If I get a good idea, they think I'm sly; if I'm tired, they call me lazy; if I eat a mouthful more than I should, I'm branded as selfish, etc., etc., etc.

I would like to ask God to give me a different nature, but that can't be done. I've got the nature that has been given to me and I'm sure it can't be bad.

Friday, 23 July, 1943
Dear Kitty,

Just for fun I'm going to tell you each person's first wish when we can go outside again. Peter wants to go into town and see a movie. His father and my sister both long more than anything for a hot bath filled to overflowing and want to stay in it for half an hour.

Peter's mother wants most to go and eat cream cakes. The dentist who lives with us wants to see his wife, who was lucky enough to be out of the country when war broke out. Mommy wants a cup of coffee, and Daddy wants to see a certain friend.

Most of all, I long for a home of our own where I am able to move freely and have help with my work again at last. In other words—school.

Saturday, 12 February, 1944
Dear Kitty,

The sun is shining, the sky is a deep blue. There is a lovely breeze, and I'm longing—so longing—for everything. To talk, for freedom, for friends, to be alone. I feel as if I'm going to burst. I'm restless. I go from one room to the other, breathe through the crack of a closed window, and feel my heart beating. I feel so confused. I don't know what to read, what to write, what to do. I only know that I am longing.

Saturday, 15 July, 1944
Dear Kitty,

It's really a wonder that I haven't dropped all my ideals because they seem so foolish and hard to carry out. Yet I keep them because, in spite of everything, I still believe that people are really good at heart. I see the world slowly being turned into a wilderness. I hear the thunder coming closer which will destroy us too. I can feel the pain and sadness of millions and yet, if I look up into the heavens, I think that it will all come right. The terrible way people treat each other will end, and peace and calm will return again.

Excerpts revised and adapted from *Anne Frank: The Diary of a Young Girl.* Copyright © 1952 by Otto H. Frank. Reprinted by permission of Doubleday & Company, Inc.

1 **About the Reading.** Answer these questions.

1. With whom does Anne seem to have the most trouble getting along and why does she seem to have this problem?

_____

_____

2. List five people who lived in the attic and state what they wanted to do when they could go out again.

   a. _____

   b. _____

   c. _____

   d. _____

   e. _____

3. Why isn't the dentist's wife hiding in the attic with the others?

_____

4. What is Anne Frank's belief about people?

_____

_____

What do you think?

5. Based on these parts of Anne Frank's diary, do you think she was a brave girl? Explain your answer.

_____

_____

6. If you were confined in an attic with seven other people for a long time, what do you think you would have the most trouble dealing with?

_____

7. If you were confined for a long time, what would be your first wish when you got outside again?

_____

8. Are there any ways in which Anne Frank reminds you of yourself? Explain your answer.

_____

_____

2 World War II. Use the words at the left to complete the sentences.

armed
bombed
changes
countries
declared
fifty
history
invaded
money
wounded

World War II killed more persons, cost more _____, destroyed more property, affected more people, and perhaps caused greater _____ in the way people lived than any other war in the _____ of mankind.

More than _____ countries took part in this war, and every country felt its terrible effects. The number of people killed, _____, or missing between September, 1939, and September, 1945, is so great that we don't even know the real number. Over fifteen million men in the _____ forces alone died on both sides.

On September 1, 1939, Hitler's army _____ Poland. Then in 1940, his war machine crushed five countries in three months. While Hitler attacked other _____, Japan _____ Pearl Harbor in Hawaii on December 7, 1941. The United States _____ war on both Japan and Germany at that time.

3 Cities, States, and Countries. Put the words at the left under the proper headings. Use a map, a globe, or the help of a friend if you wish.

Amsterdam
Baltimore
Boston
California
Detroit
Egypt
Germany
Hawaii
Holland
Japan
Michigan
Ohio
Rome
Spain
Washington

Cities	States	Countries
1. _____	1. _____	1. _____
2. _____	2. _____	2. _____
3. _____	3. _____	3. _____
4. _____	4. _____	4. _____
5. _____	5. _____	5. _____

4 **More Work with Word Endings.** Say the words in each group at the left out loud. Then fill in the blanks with the right answers.

nature
picture

1. The _____ on the wall reminded Peter of a _____ walk that he had taken in the state park last summer.

attic
picnic

2. Mrs. Ray asked her daughter to bring the yellow basket down from the _____ so she could pack the sandwiches for the _____.

foolish
selfish

3. It is really _____ to be _____ because we always receive so much more from others when we are kindhearted.

cattle
terrible

4. The cowboys prayed that their _____ would not be harmed by the _____ disease that was spreading throughout the state.

meadow
swallow

5. Mark decided to _____ his pride and let the baseball team that had beaten his team so badly have their yearly picnic in his _____.

chemical
total

6. The president said that the _____ cost of the new wing for the _____ plant would be three billion dollars.

baggage
manager
message

7. The _____ left a _____ for the angry hotel guests in which he informed them that their _____ was coming in on the next plane.

kindness
sadness
wilderness

8. The fact that we have not treated the _____ with much _____ fills many people with great _____.

Lesson 14

The Ship of the Desert

Tony Allegretti

Victor Englebert

Words for Study

camel	clumsy	trait	shrubs
Africa	hump	protected	blankets
cargo	humpbacked	overhanging	produce
Texas	stupid	lashes	full-grown
shaggy	among	nostrils	curdle

The Ship of the Desert

The camel is a huge, ugly desert animal who can go hundreds of miles across hot, dry deserts with little food or water. For thousands of years, people have depended upon the camel to carry them across the great deserts of Asia and Africa. For this reason, the camel has been named "the ship of the desert."

Even the United States has tried using camels. In the 1850's, the army brought about eighty camels from Africa and Asia to carry cargo from Texas to California. However, the railroads, which were being built then, could carry cargo faster and cheaper than camels could. As a result, the army sold most of the camels to circuses and zoos.

The camel will never win a prize for good looks. It is a shaggy, clumsy, humpbacked beast. It has a split upper lip; its eyes look as if they're about ready to pop out of its head; its jaw is loose; and its face is too small. The face looks somewhat sad and stupid.

Yet, this face is very well suited to life on the desert. The eyes are protected from the sun by overhanging lids and long lashes. The nostrils can close up tightly against the driving sand of desert storms. The camel's upper lip can reach out for the shrubs and other plants which it eats. Its strong, yellow teeth can chew nearly anything. The two-humped camel will even eat leather, blankets, and bones.

The most outstanding trait of the camel's body is the hump or humps on the middle of its back. The hump weighs eighty pounds or more, which is about 1/20 of the animal's entire weight. The camel stores most of its fat inside its hump. The hump is not used to store water as some people believe. Camels drink huge amounts of water (one camel drank thirty gallons in ten minutes) because there is no place in the camel's body to store it.

It takes about eleven months to produce a baby camel. From their fourth year, camels are taught to kneel, rise, and carry heavy loads. The camel has pads on its chest and knees to protect the rest of its body from the sand when it is kneeling. Its two-toed feet are also padded to keep it from sinking into the soft sand. A camel is not full-grown until it is seventeen years old, and it lives thirty or forty years.

Even though there is no such thing as a wild camel, the camel is not exactly tame. For example, the camel is never really a willing worker. It will bite, kick, and whine with or without cause. The camel has a sad and moody temper and often displays fits of anger. The moodiness of a camel is so bad that it has few friends, even among other camels.

The camel may only be able to go two and a half miles an hour, but he can make twenty-five miles a day with a load on his hump of up to a thousand pounds. The camel is also useful because his hair is used to make cloth, fine blankets, and tents. The skin can be made into very good leather. Also, the camel produces milk. Just don't ever put any camel's milk into your coffee or tea, however, because it will curdle at once.

1 **About the Reading.** Answer these questions.

1. What is "the ship of the desert"? _____

2. In what two places in the world do people depend upon these animals?

   _____ and _____

3. What is stored in the camel's hump or humps? _____

4. At what age is a camel a full-grown animal? _____

5. List three reasons that explain how the camel's face is suited to life on the desert.

   a. _____

   b. _____

   c. _____

6. How far can a camel go in a day? _____

7. How much can a camel carry at one time? _____

8. List three things that people use camels for besides getting themselves from place to place.

   a. _____

   b. _____

   c. _____

9. Why would a camel make a poor pet? _____

   _____

What do you think?

10. Which animal do you think makes the best pet? Be sure to give at least one reason
    for your answer.

    _____

    _____

2 Compound Words.

To find the answers to these clues, choose a word from **List A** and add a word from **List B** to it. Study the example before you begin.

List A	List B
bee	back
bird	bite
dog	bowl
✓duck	hole
fish	house
fox	line
monkey	✓pin
mouse	shines
pig	skin
piggy	tail
sheep	trap
snake	wood

duckpin   1. This bowling pin is shorter and fatter than a tenpin.

_____ 2. This is a long braid or braids of hair hanging at the back of the head.

_____ 3. This straight line gets its name from the belief that a bee flies straight back to its hive after getting nectar.

_____ 4. Men in the army dig this in order to be safe from guns fired by the other side.

_____ 5. People buy this at a hardware store to get rid of mice.

_____ 6. This is the bite of a snake.

_____ 7. This describes carrying someone on your shoulders.

_____ 8. This is a family of small trees and shrubs that produce lovely flowers.

_____ 9. This is made out of glass and is used to keep small fish, snails, etc.

_____ 10. This is a small box, like a house, for birds to live in.

_____ 11. This is used for coats or leather and is often used to make certain kinds of paper for important matters.

_____ 12. This word describes tricks or jokes played on other people.

3 **More Work with Word Endings.** Say the words in each group at the left out loud. Then fill in the blanks with the right answers.

blanket
bracelet

1. Thinking that her pearl _____ was somewhere on the bed, Mary

shook out the _____ in hopes that she would find it.

produce
reduce

2. In order to _____ more work at a faster rate, the manager decided

to _____ the size of his working force and buy new machines.

Africa
America

3. The first slaves were brought to _____ from _____ in the year 1619.

camels
channel

4. On _____ 4 last night, there was a movie in which all the main

actors rode _____ .

curdled
paddle

5. The farmer told his son that if he found _____ milk in the pail

again, he would _____ him so hard that his son wouldn't be able to sit down for a week.

borrow
narrow

6. After a _____ escape from the burning building, the fireman

wanted to _____ money to phone his wife.

affected
collected
rejected

7. Herman was so _____ when the manager _____ him

from the starting line-up that he _____ his things and left the stadium at once.

chickens
dozen
heaven's
kitchen

8. "What in _____ name are a _____ _____

doing in my _____ !" exclaimed Kate.

4 **Syllables.** Each of the words listed below has more than one syllable. Write the syllables on the lines to the right. If a vowel is underlined, mark it either long or short.

1. carg_o_   _____ • _____

2. curdle   _____ • _____

3. sh_a_ggy   _____ • _____

4. k_i_ndn_e_ss   _____ • _____

5. c_o_nf_u_se   _____ • _____

6. th_u_nder   _____ • _____

7. fr_ee_ly   _____ • _____

8. att_a_ck   _____ • _____

9. German   _____ • _____

10. office   _____ • _____

11. _i_nm_a_te   _____ • _____

12. perh_a_ps   _____ • _____

13. _u_np_a_ck   _____ • _____

14. H_o_lland   _____ • _____

15. _A_msterd_a_m   _____ • _____ • _____

16. _o_verhanging   _____ • _____ • _____ • _____

Lesson 15

Some Facts about Southpaws

Words for Study

southpaws	patterns	hookers	handicapped
culture	flints	uncommon	bicycle
left-handed	regarded	lob	handle
right-handed	students	misfit	farewell

Some Facts about Southpaws

No culture has ever been left-handed. Even the people who lived in the Stone Age were right-handed. We know this because the patterns of skull wounds in apes killed for food by the cavemen show that most of the blows were struck with the right hand. Also, flints and other tools made by cavemen were for use by right-handed people.

For hundreds of years, people who are left-handed have been regarded as either bad or crazy. In 1903, a man in Italy who studied crime for a living wrote a book in which he claimed that the jails were filled with left-handed people. Until the 1930's in the United States, most children were forced to write with their right hand. Any child who was found writing with his left hand was normally slapped hard on the hand with a ruler. The classroom atmosphere is more peaceful now for southpaws, and it is said that about one out of every six or seven students is left-handed.

Far more men than women are left-handed. Left-handed men tend to be "hookers." A "hooker" is a term used to describe a person who writes with the point of the pen down and his hand above the line of writing. Most left-handed women write with their hand below the writing line.

Right-handed people do almost all tasks with their right hand. Left-handed people tend to use both hands. For example, it is not at all uncommon to see a left-handed person lob a basketball, mend socks, or perform other tasks with his right hand.

In spite of the fact that about twenty million people in the United States alone are left-handed, some people continue to believe that southpaws aren't as smart as right-handed people. It is true that a higher number of left-handed people stutter or have learning problems. It's also true that more misfits in our culture are left-handed. However, when you remember that our culture is geared to the needs of the right-handed person, is it any wonder that a left-handed person is going to have some problems learning how to do things?

Nobody really knows why some people are left-handed. One doctor believes that southpaws become left-handed either before birth or during birth. According to this doctor, the left side of the brain, which controls the right hand, needs more oxygen than the right side. If there is not enough oxygen, then the right side of the brain is called upon, and the baby will be left-handed.

Not everybody agrees with this doctor's ideas. Some people don't agree because they think the doctor is saying that left-handed people are handicapped. Others disagree with the "lack of oxygen" idea because they believe that a person gets his right-handed or left-handed traits from his mother and father.

Those who are studying left-handed people today aren't so nutty as the man from Italy who claimed that left-handed people are bad, but they really don't know much more about this whole subject than he did.

Adapted with permission from the March 1979 *Reader's Digest*.
Copyright © 1979 by the Reader's Digest Association Inc.
"Is It Sinister to Be Left-Handed?" by Jack Fincher.

1 **About the Reading.** Answer these questions.

1. Fill in the blanks with the right answers.

   a. The nickname for people who are left-handed is _____.

   b. The man who wrote a book in which he stated that left-handed people are bad was

   from the country _____.

   c. He wrote this book in the year _____.

   d. A _____ writes with the point of the pen down and his hand above the line of writing.

   e. About _____ people in the United States alone are left-handed.

   f. Our culture is geared to the needs of the _____ person.

   g. The _____ side of the brain controls the right hand.

   h. One doctor believes that a person is left-handed because of a lack of _____ either before or during birth.

2. True or false? Write *true* if the statement agrees with what you just read. Write *false* if the statement disagrees with what you just read.

   _____ a. It is not known whether cavemen were right-handed or left-handed.

   _____ b. Left-handed children used to be treated badly in school.

   _____ c. Left-handed people tend to use both hands when performing tasks.

   _____ d. No culture has ever been left-handed.

   _____ e. There is wide disagreement about the cause of left-handed traits.

   _____ f. Most people who are left-handed are women.

   _____ g. Right-handed people use their left hands just as much as they use their right hands to perform tasks.

   _____ h. Most left-handed people have problems because the culture is geared to the needs of right-handed people.

   _____ i. The doctor who formed the "lack of oxygen" idea thinks that left-handed people are handicapped.

   _____ j. There are still people today who think that left-handed people aren't as good as right-handed people.

2 **"Handy" Sayings.** Write the letter of the best answer on the line.

_____ 1. Which of these sayings would a cop or robber be likely to use?

   (a) "Hands down."   (c) "Hands up."
   (b) "Hands off."   (d) "Join hands."

_____ 2. Which of these sayings would a selfish person be likely to use?

   (a) "Hands off."   (c) "Join hands."
   (b) "In hand."   (d) "Out of hand."

_____ 3. Which of these sayings describes a busy person?

   (a) "force one's hand"   (c) "not lift a hand"
   (b) "have one's hands full"   (d) "turn one's hand to"

_____ 4. If something "gets out of hand," it's _____.

   (a) no longer in control   (c) on the floor
   (b) no longer owned by you   (d) taken over by machines

_____ 5. Which one of these terms shows agreement rather than disagreement?

   (a) "out of hand"   (c) "on the other hand"
   (b) "hands off"   (d) "hand in hand"

_____ 6. How would most people like to make money?

   (a) "from hand to hand"   (c) "out of hand"
   (b) "hand over fist"   (d) "with a heavy hand"

_____ 7. If someone asks you to help with the dishes, and you "don't lift a hand," you're _____.

   (a) handicapped   (c) not even trying to help out
   (b) not able to find a towel   (d) not sure what to do

_____ 8. If you have someone "eating out of your hand," _____.

   (a) you'd better wash your hands   (c) he is rude
   (b) he is hungry   (d) he is controlled by you

3 **"Handy" Words.** Match the words at the left with the statements that best define them. Sound out the words you have not studied using the rules you know.

handbag

handball

handcuff

handful

handle

handlebar

handpick

handshake

handsome

handy

_____ 1. This is a curved or bent bar used for steering a bicycle.

_____ 2. This is a game in which a small ball is batted against a wall or walls with the hand.

_____ 3. This is the gripping and shaking of another's hand in greeting, farewell, agreement, etc.

_____ 4. This is a small container for money, lipstick, keys, etc.

_____ 5. This is as much as the hand will hold.

_____ 6. This is either of a pair of connected steel rings that can be locked about the wrists.

_____ 7. This means good-looking.

_____ 8. This is the part of a tool which is held, turned, or pulled with the hand.

_____ 9. This means useful or near at hand.

_____ 10. This means to choose with care for a certain reason.

4 **Singular and Plural Words.** Write the singular words listed below under the heading marked **Singular**. To the right of the singular form, write the plural form. Study the example before you begin.

✓ leaf

lashes

diaries

half

employer

ox

bicycles

lash

cattle

deer

diary

units

employers

bicycle

✓ leaves

unit

cow

halves

oxen

deer

	Singular	Plural
1.	*leaf*	*leaves*
2.		
3.		
4.		
5.		
6.		
7.		
8.		
9.		
10.		

Review: Lessons 1-15

1 **Answer These Questions.** Fill in the blanks with the right answers.

_____ 1. Who was the ruler of Germany during World War II? (Include his first and last names.)

_____ 2. In what year did World War II end?

_____ 3. Name another country besides Germany that the United States fought in this war.

_____ 4. What is the name of the girl whose World War II diary you read?

_____ 5. In what country did her family hide from the Germans?

_____ 6. What animal is often called the "ship of the desert"?

_____ 7. In what two places in the world do people depend on this animal?

_____ 8. What is inside a camel's hump?

_____ 9. What is the nickname given to left-handed people?

_____ 10. About how many people in the United States are left-handed?

2 **Word Study.** Choose the right answer from the four choices and write it on the line.

_____ 1. To lob a ball is to _____.
  (a) kick it fast   (c) throw it fast
  (b) kick it slowly   (d) throw it high

_____ 2. Small children often call their toes _____.
  (a) bunnies   (b) camels   (c) kitties   (d) piggies

_____ 3. Pearl Harbor is in _____.
  (a) Germany   (b) Japan   (c) Poland   (d) the United States

_____ 4. History is the study of man's _____.
  (a) ideals   (b) nature   (c) past   (d) traits

_____ 5. _____ fever is one kind of disease.
  (a) blue   (b) red   (c) white   (d) yellow

_____ 6. Nostrils are used mainly for _____.
  (a) breathing   (b) showing anger   (c) sneezing   (d) talking

_____ 7. A flint is used mainly to _____.

       (a) crack a skull   (c) kill an ape

       (b) draw a picture   (d) start a fire

_____ 8. A person who tends to destroy the fun that others are having is called a _____ blanket.

       (a) cold   (b) moldy   (c) moist   (d) wet

_____ 9. When milk curdles, it becomes _____.

       (a) gas   (b) liquid   (c) solid   (d) chocolate

_____ 10. The ideas, traits, skills, and arts of a certain people define their _____.

       (a) beliefs   (b) culture   (c) handicaps   (d) patterns

3 **Matching.** Match each item at the left with the statement that best defines it.

A.M.	_____	1. a man
B.C.		
Dr.	_____	2. a statement of owing money
etc.	_____	3. a woman who is either married or not married
IOU		
Mr.	_____	4. a woman who is married
Mrs.	_____	5. and so forth
Ms.		
	_____	6. before noon
	_____	7. doctor
	_____	8. the time before Christ's birth

4 **Matching.** Match each word at the left with the right country.

American	_____	1. England
Dutch		
English	_____	2. France
French	_____	3. Germany
German		
Greek	_____	4. Greece
	_____	5. Holland
	_____	6. United States

5 **Meet Ms. Brown.** Choose the right answer for each sentence from the words listed at the left. Take your time!

accepting
clumsy
confused
foolish
handicapped
kindhearted
lazy
loneliness
moody
selfish

1. Ms. Brown was so _____ that she would go out of her way to help just about anybody.

2. The only people she didn't offer her help to were _____ people who just sat around all day doing nothing.

3. These people would always call Ms. Brown _____ when she said NO! to their demands.

4. Ms. Brown would always reply, "God helps those who help themselves," and wonder how people could be so _____ as to waste their entire lives.

5. Every Wednesday, Ms. Brown spent three hours at a center that had just been opened for _____ people.

6. When they first came to the center, these people would often act _____ because they had trouble _____ the fact that they had a handicap.

7. Often they were _____ because they hadn't yet gotten used to their crutches or other aids.

8. Ms. Brown was _____ about what to do. She wanted to help them through their _____, but she knew that they had to get used to their handicap and the center on their own terms.

6 **Spelling Check.** The answers for the clues are listed at the left. As you can see, the letters of the words are all mixed up. Spell the words the right way on the lines.

1. a d H l l n o   _____ The city Amsterdam is in this country.

2. a e s T x   _____ This is the second largest state in the United States.

3. l r t u y   _____ Many people sign their letters "Yours _____."

4. a e g s w   _____ The main reason many workers decide to strike is that they want higher _____.

5. a d i o r   _____ Many people have this on while they're driving their automobiles.

6. e d i n s t t _____ You sit in a chair while he drills your teeth.

7. d e n s t t u _____ This person works at a desk or table and is given homework by a teacher.

8. a e G m n r y _____ This country was split into East _____ and West _____ after World War II.

7 **More Work with Syllables.** Write the syllables of each word on the lines to the right.

1. handcuff _____ • _____

2. protect _____ • _____

3. pigtail _____ • _____

4. statement _____ • _____

5. therefore _____ • _____

6. depress _____ • _____

7. beeline _____ • _____

8. itself _____ • _____

9. fishbowl _____ • _____

10. duckpin _____ • _____

11. loneliness _____ • _____ • _____

12. uncommon _____ • _____ • _____

13. wilderness _____ • _____ • _____

14. misfit _____ • _____

15. agreement _____ • _____ • _____

16. disagreement _____ • _____ • _____ • _____

A

accept
action
Adolf
affect
Africa
agreement
airplane
Al
A.M.
America
American
among
amount
Amsterdam
anyone
apple
artery
Asia
atmosphere
attack
attic
aware
ax(e)

B

Babe
baggage
baggy
balloon
Baltimore
Bambino
basement
battery
battleship
beam
beeline
beginning
belief
believer
belly
belonging
berry
bicycle
bidder
bidding
billionth
birdhouse
blanket
blender
blindness
boring
borrow
bottom
boxcar
boxing
brandy

breadboard
breather
breezy
broiler
bubble
built
bully
bunny
bushy
butterfly
buzzer

C

camel
carbon
carbon dioxide
cargo
Carver, G.W.
carving
cattle
caveman
channel
chat
chemical
choosy
choppy
Christmas Eve
clammy
cloudburst
clumsy
coating
collect
color
coloring
concept
conduct
conductor
connect
continue
cooky
cranberry
creamy
crisp
crossing
crudely
culture
curdle
curly

D

daring
dashboard
deaf
deafness
dealer
degree
depress
desert

diagram
dial
diary
digger
dining
disagreement
disc
disease
dishwasher
dogwood
downward
dozen
drawing
drummer
duckpin
dusty

E

easiness
Edison, T.
effect
entire
escape
exhale

F

farewell
fatty
feeler
fever
fishbowl
flicker
flint
flipper
floorboard
floppy
flowery
foolish
forest
foxhole
frank
Frank
freely
friendship
full-grown

G

gearshift
German
Germany
god
good-looking
grasshopper
gravy
greasy
growth
gummy
gunner

H

hailstone
half-hour
hamburger
handball
handcuff
handicap
handle
handlebar
handpick
handshake
handsome
harbor
Hawaii
heap
hearing
heaven
Herman
hero
high-priced
hiker
history
Hitler, A.
holiday
Holland
hooker
hot dog
hump
humpbacked
hungry
Huron

I

ideal
ill-mannered
immense
inch
Indian
inmate
inning
insider
inspect
inspector
intermission
invader
invention
inventor
Italy
item
itself

J

jackhammer
Japan
Jewish
jog
jogger

jogging
Johnson
jumper

K

killer
kindhearted
kindness

L

ladybug
lash
latch
laziness
leafy
league
learner
lefthanded
lightly
likely
liner
line-up
lob
locate
locker
logger
loneliness
lying

M

make-believe
manners
matting
M.D.
meadow
medicine
menu
merging
message
meteor
meteorite
Michigan
milkshake
mining
misfit
monkeyshines
moodiness
moody
moonlight
moonshine
mound
mousetrap
mousy
mouthpart
movement
muggy
museum
mustn't

N

narrow
nature
nervy
nevertheless
normal
normally
North Pole
nostril

O

object
offer
office
officer
Ohio
one-fourth
one-third
orange
outline
outsider
overhanging
overheard
oxen
oxygen

P

pacemaker
paddle
padlock
panty
pasty
patter
pattern
pearl
Pearl Harbor
peppy
per
perform
performer
perhaps
Peter
picnic
piggyback
pigtail
planet
pleasing
plural
pocket
Poland
pollen
polo
potty
prayer
pretend
printer

process
produce
program
prompt
prong
protect
Pueblo

Q

R
racket
radio
railway
rainstorm
ray
reader
reading
receive
reflect
regard
release
result
rigging

righthanded
runner
rusty

S
salad
sandpaper
sandy
Santa Claus
scaly
scary
screwdriver
selfish
setting
shaggy
shaker
sheepskin
shortcut
shred
shrub
silky
singular
skipper

skylight
skyline
skyscraper
slop
sloppy
smoggy
snakebite
snapper
soapy
soupspoon
southpaw
South Pole
southwest
sox
speedy
spelling
spider
spongy
squish
stadium
starfish
statement
steal

steer
stomp
strainer
strawberry
string bean
stroll
student
stupid
sudden
sunflower
sunstroke
suntan
swallow
swamp
swirl

T
tennis
tenpin
termite
terrible
Texas
therefore

they've
Thomas
thunder
tiny
toe
Tommy
tongue
topping
total
trader
training
trait
truly
tuner
turkey
TV

U
unaware
uncommon
upper
upward
used

V
vein
view

W
waitress
washer
watcher
wheezy
whiskey
widely
wilderness
wind
wiper
World War II
worry
worship

X

Y
Yankee
yellow

Z

Lesson 16

Some Thoughts about Dying

Words for Study

dying	differently	hormones	despite
aside	backyard	opium	distress
details	blight	prove	fully
step-by-step	wince	accident	beneath

Some Thoughts about Dying

There are so many books about dying that bookstores and libraries have set aside whole shelves for them. Some of these books are so packed with details and step-by-step lessons for dying that you'd think this was a new sort of skill which all of us are now required to learn. Also, these books could lead you to believe that only human beings are aware of death and that all the rest of nature dies differently from people.

An elm tree in our backyard caught the blight this summer and dropped stone dead almost overnight. One weekend it was a normal elm tree, and the next weekend it was dead.

The dying of a field mouse at the jaws of a friendly household cat is a sight I have seen many times. It used to make me wince. Early in life, I gave up throwing sticks at the cat to make him drop the mouse because the dropped mouse went ahead and died anyway.

Lately, I've done some thinking about that mouse. I wonder if his dying is really all that different from the death of our elm tree. The main difference, if there is one, would be in the matter of pain. I do not believe that an elm tree feels the pain of a mouse hanging from the teeth of a gray cat.

But does the mouse feel pain? There are now some reasons for thinking it does not feel much pain at all. At the time of being trapped and bitten by the cat's teeth, hormones are released by cells in two glands. These cells have the properties of opium, so there is no pain. Perhaps that is why the mouse always seems to hang so calmly from the cat's jaws. He's so calm, in fact, that when dropped, he dies of his wounds without a struggle. I do not know if this is true or not, nor do I know how to prove it if it is true.

A French writer had a hunch about dying based on his own close call in a riding accident. He was so badly hurt that he was believed to be dead by his friends who, crying, carried him home. The writer remembers everything despite having been "dead" for two full hours:

"It seemed to me that my life was hanging only by the tip of my lips. I closed my eyes in order to help push it out and enjoyed growing calm and letting myself go. It was an idea that was not only free from distress, but also joined with that sweet feeling that people have who have let themselves slide into sleep . . . In order to get used to the idea of death, I find there is nothing like coming close to it . . . If you do not know how to die, never trouble yourself. Nature will, in a moment, fully teach you. She will do that business for you exactly. Take no care for it."

Pain is useful, but when it is the end game and no way back, pain is likely to be turned off, and the way in which this is done is sure and quick. In a world in which people and animals have to live off each other and in which dying is a part of living, I cannot think of a better way it could be.

1 **About the Reading.** Choose the letter of the best answer and put it on the line to the left.

_____ 1. According to the writer, people living today _____
(a) are reading more about dying than ever before.
(b) are scared of dying.
(c) never think about dying.
(d) think about dying only when death is near.

_____ 2. Blight is _____
(a) a disease.   (b) a kind of insect.   (c) death.   (d) the cold.

_____ 3. The "end game" in this reading means _____
(a) accidents.   (b) dying.   (c) nature.   (d) pain.

_____ 4. At first, the writer thinks that a mouse might feel _____ than a tree while dying.
(a) more lonely   (b) sadder   (c) more pain   (d) more afraid

_____ 5. Then the writer wonders if the mouse _____
(a) deserves to die.
(b) doesn't understand that it is dying.
(c) feels any pain at all.
(d) is really as calm as it looks during its last moments.

6. The French writer quoted in this reading thinks that _____
   (a) dying is a painful experience.
   (b) life is mainly in your lips.
   (c) nature takes over during a person's last moments.
   (d) you should read as much as you can about dying.

7. The writer _____ his ideas.
   (a) can prove
   (b) cannot prove
   (c) does not think it is important to prove
   (d) knows how to prove

8. The writer thinks that _____
   (a) he could improve upon nature.
   (b) he could not improve upon nature.
   (c) people should not have to be in pain.
   (d) pain is useless.

9. According to the writer, _____ kill pain just before death.
   (a) cats   (b) cells   (c) glands   (d) hormones

10. The writer seems to enjoy _____
    (a) museums.   (b) nature.   (c) sports.   (d) summer.

2 **About the Reading.** Put these statements in the order in which the writer believes they happen during the process of death.

— The living thing becomes calm.
— A living thing is badly hurt.
— There is no pain.
— Death happens without a struggle.
— Hormones are released.

1. _____

2. _____

3. _____

4. _____

5. _____

3 **The Ending -ly.** Rewrite each word on the line to the right and add *ly* to it. Then use these words to complete the sentences below. Study the example before you begin.

different _____   awful _____

narrow _*narrowly*_____   nervous _____

sudden _____   entire _____

foolish _____   strict _____

most _____   prompt _____

1. After _*narrowly*___ escaping from the sinking cargo ship, the thankful sailors were picked up by the United States Coast Guard.

2. Before going to her hotel room, Mrs. Thomas asked the desk clerk to call her

   _____ at seven o'clock, so she wouldn't be late for her sales meeting.

3. The people were not _____ happy with the president because he had not followed through on his pledge to lower taxes.

4. Herb _____ tapped his foot as he waited for the doctor to give him the results of his daughter's blood tests.

5. The Carver boy _____ left his bicycle beneath the tree during the rainstorm; the next morning, he found that the handlebars had already begun to rust.

6. The inspector on the day shift went _____ by the rules, but the inspector on the evening shift seemed to let the workers he really liked get away with murder.

7. The judge was just about to make a statement when, _____, a strange woman rose from her seat in the back of the courtroom and confessed that she had committed the crime.

8. During the winter she used her car _____ for going to work, but in the summer she also used it to drive to the beach four times a week.

9. When Ben begged his father to give him a piggyback ride, his father replied, "I just got home

   from work, and I'm _____ tired—maybe later, after dinner."

10. Just because others do things _____ from the way we're used to doing them doesn't mean that we're right and they're wrong.

4 **More Work with the Ending -*ly*.** Change the *y* to *i* and add -*ly* to these words. Study the example before you begin.

1. easy _easily_   5. unlucky _____

2. body _____   6. speedy _____

3. busy _____   7. happy _____

4. greedy _____   8. clumsy _____

5 **More Work with Compound Words.** Choose the best answer and write it on the line so each sentence makes sense. (Use the rules you have studied to sound out the new words.)

1. The reporter didn't know whether she would be able to meet the _____ for her story about the Pine Tree Camping Club.
   (a) beeline   (b) deadline   (c) pipeline   (d) streamline

2. She had first heard about the camping club's latest trip while waiting in line to buy the morning paper at the _____.
   (a) newscast   (b) newsletter   (c) newsreel   (d) newsstand

3. The reporter _____ one woman complaining to her friend about an awful camping trip she and her family had just returned from.
   (a) overcrowded   (b) overheard   (c) overloaded   (d) overturned

4. It seemed that the manager of the _____ had led the Pine Tree Camping Club to believe his place was much finer than it really was.
   (a) background   (b) battleground   (c) campground   (d) playground

5. When the reporter questioned the woman, she admitted that the camping club should have known it was in for a bad time because the manager had sent them such an old map that they had gotten lost seven times after getting off the _____.
   (a) freeborn   (b) freeform   (c) freeload   (d) freeway

6. Then, after _____, the club suddenly became aware of the fact that the only light they would have was their flashlights.
   (a) sunrise   (b) sunset   (c) sunshine   (d) sunstroke

7. The woman, whose name was Mrs. Lee, agreed to give the reporter more details about the terrible camp at the _____ coffee shop.
   (a) brotherhood   (b) childhood   (c) neighborhood   (d) sisterhood

8. After the waitress had taken their order, Mrs. Lee gave the reporter the

   _____ on the camp.
   (a) comedown   (b) countdown   (c) lowdown   (d) sundown

9. "Not only did we have to pitch our tents on rocky ground," complained Mrs. Lee,

   "we had to listen to _____ all day because they were building a
   high-rise right down the road!"
   (a) jackhammers   (b) jackknife   (c) jackpots   (d) jackstraw

10. "But," she exclaimed, "the worst thing of all was the total lack of bathrooms. We

   had to use _____!"
   (a) clubhouses   (b) greenhouses   (c) hothouses   (d) outhouses

Lesson 17

The Number One Eater in America

The Bettmann Archive

Words for Study

eater	muffins	soda	restaurant
James B. Brady	midmorning	bartender	customers
bellhop	oysters	turtle	P.M.
"Diamond Jim"	crabs	vegetables	champagne
collector	lobsters	ma'am	hospital
jewelry	bottles	stomach	Atlantic City

The Number One Eater in America

You will not find James B. Brady's name in American history books, but the fact remains that he is perhaps the country's number one eater of all times. Born in 1856, Brady was first hired as a bellhop at a hotel where he spent as much time eating as he did working. He then went on to become an extremely successful salesman.

Brady became known as "Diamond Jim." This nickname came from the fact that he was a collector of diamond jewelry. His jewelry was said to be worth two million dollars. "Diamond Jim" spent as much time eating as he spent working and collecting diamond jewelry.

Just what was a normal eating day for Diamond Jim Brady? Well, for breakfast he would start off with a full gallon of orange juice. Then came eggs, corn bread, muffins, pancakes, chops, fried potatoes, and a steak. This would hold him until about 11:30 A.M. when he would have his midmorning snack—two or three dozen clams and oysters.

An hour later, Diamond Jim was ready for lunch. First more oysters and clams, then two or three crabs, next a platter of lobsters, followed by a joint of beef, a salad, and many different kinds of pie. During the afternoon came another snack followed by lots of bottles of lemon soda. Jim, the son of a bartender, never touched whiskey. After lying down for an hour or two, Jim was ready for dinner.

To begin his dinner, Diamond Jim would often eat two or three dozen oysters. Then would follow half a dozen crabs, claws and all. After the crabs, there was a short pause for two helpings of green turtle soup and six or seven huge lobsters. Next came two whole ducks, a steak and vegetables.

Last, of course, came dessert. Diamond Jim chose his desserts in handfuls. When he pointed to a platter of French treats, he didn't mean just one piece of cake or pie. He meant the whole platter. The meal would conclude with Jim's ordering a two-pound box of candy which he would then pass around among his guests at the dining table. Jim would order another two-pound box just for himself. "They make the food set better," he declared.

A woman once asked Diamond Jim how he knew when he was full. "Why, ma'am, I'll tell you," Brady replied. "Whenever I sit down to a meal, I always make it a point to leave just four inches between my stomach and the edge of the table. And then, when I can feel them rubbing together pretty hard, I *know* I've had enough." Most of Diamond Jim's eating was done out. One restaurant owner claimed that he was "the best twenty-five customers we had."

Jim was no slouch when it came to throwing parties either. Once, in honor of his race horse Golden Heels, he invited fifty friends to a dinner at a New York restaurant. There, between 4 P.M. and 9 P.M., more than five hundred bottles of champagne were consumed, not to mention many steaks and desserts. All told, the party set Brady back more than $100,000!

In the end, the strain told. At fifty-six, Jim was taken to the hospital where it was learned that his stomach was six times as large as a normal person's. When told that he could, with proper eating, live ten more years, Diamond Jim exclaimed, "Who wants to live ten more years if he has to do all them things?" Five years later, on April 16, 1917, Diamond Jim Brady died at a hotel in Atlantic City. He went down eating.

1 **About the Reading.** Answer these questions.

1. Give the dates of Diamond Jim Brady's life.

_____ to _____

2. How did Diamond Jim earn his living? _____

3. How did Diamond Jim get his nickname?

_____

4. What did Diamond Jim have in mind when he pointed to a platter of desserts?

_____

5. How did Diamond Jim know when he had had enough to eat?

_____

6. What advice did the doctors give Diamond Jim?

_____

7. Why didn't Jim listen to the doctors' warning?

_____

8. Where did Diamond Jim die and what was the cause of his death?

_____

What do you think?

9. Diamond Jim refused to give up his way of eating. Give another common example of how people refuse to take doctors' advice and continue to do what they want to do.

_____

_____

2 **Food for Thought.** The words at the left are used to describe things other than food. Use these words to complete the ten sentences.

apple
beef
bread
cheese
chicken
crab
dough
honey
lemon
toast

1. New York City is often called "the Big _____."

2. Something you buy that doesn't work right is called a _____.

3. Sometimes, if a person loses his nerve, he is called a _____.

4. The act of drinking to a person's health or honor is called a _____.

5. A slang word for money is _____.

6. Another slang word for money is _____.

7. A slang word for a complaint that you have is _____.

8. You might call somebody you like very, very much "_____."

9. A _____ is a person who has nasty things to say about everything and everybody.

10. When you're having your picture taken, you're often asked to say,

"_____."

3 **The Ending** *-ful.* Rewrite each word on the line to the right and add *-ful* to it. Then use these words to complete the sentences below. Study the example before you begin.

bag _____   shame _____

color _*colorful*_____   spite _____

delight _____   success _____

faith _____   tear _____

grace _____   wish _____

respect _____   wonder _____

1. Many people think that autumn is the most _*colorful*_____ season of the year.

2. Can you sing all four verses of "O, Come All Ye _____"?

3. If you are not _____ at first, do you give up, or do you try again?

4. Jim wanted a raise so he could make the down payment on a new car, but he knew this was

   just _____ thinking.

5. Mike was just being _____ when he refused to phone Ruth and tell her he was sorry that he had completely forgotten her birthday.

6. Most children in the United States are taught to think that on Christmas Eve Santa Claus

   rides in a sleigh with a huge _____ of toys.

7. Billy became _____ as he broke down and told his wife how the pitching coach had screamed at him all throughout spring training.

8. Diamond Jim Brady was being _____ when he called the woman who asked him a question in the restaurant "ma'am."

9. Mr. James told his wife that it was _____ to spend so much money on a dress that she planned to wear only once.

10. The Scotts had such a _____ evening at the restaurant that they decided to eat there again next Friday.

11. Dennis' dive was so _____ that the judges all agreed he should receive first prize.

12. The birth of a child is a _____ thing.

4 **Working with Syllables.** In the box are syllables which are used to make words. The words match with the ten sentences below. No syllable is used twice, and no syllable should be left over when you are done. The number next to the sentence tells you how many syllables are in each right answer. Study the example before you begin.

ad	ber	~~bles~~	break	choc	dough	~~e~~	fast	ghet	gurt
la	late	men	nil	nuts	o	oys	rant	res	ry	sal
spa	straw	~~ta~~	tau	ter	ti	u	va	~~veg~~	yo

vegetables   1. Beets, peas, string beans, and potatoes are _____. (4)

_____ 2. Fishermen always hope to find a pearl in one of these. (2)

_____ 3. Many people believe this snack or dessert is very healthy for you. (2)

_____ 4. Many workers like to eat these during their coffee break. (2)

_____ 5. Most people toss this with some kind of dressing before they eat it. (2)

_____ 6. One kind of ice cream is _____. (3)

_____ 7. Another kind of ice cream is _____. (3)

_____ 8. Still another kind of ice cream is _____. (3)

_____ 9. This is where people go when they want to go out for dinner. (3)

_____ 10. This is often served with meatballs and tomato sauce on it. (3)

_____ 11. The waiter gives each person a _____, so he can decide what to order. (2)

_____ 12. Many people believe this is the most important meal of the day. (2)

Lesson 18

The Great Hunger

Library of Congress

Words for Study

hunger	spade	cabbage	island
Ireland	dangerous	suffered	grandchildren
hardship	clearly	flee	conditions
county	stank	Irish	mountains
acre	faintly	fled	New Hampshire

The Great Hunger

Life in Ireland in the 1800's was filled with hardship. A well-known duke had once said, "There never was a country in which the poor exist to the extent that they exist in Ireland." There is much proof that the duke was right. For example, in 1837, it was learned that one county in Ireland had 9,000 people but only ten beds and ninety-three chairs. Pigs slept with their owners, and people who had no homes at all lived in ditches.

Just about everybody in Ireland depended on the potato for food. An acre and a half of potatoes was enough to keep a family of five or six alive for one year. Also, only a spade was needed to grow potatoes. The people did not need to buy a lot of costly tools which they couldn't have afforded anyway. The people not only ate the potatoes themselves, but also fed them to the pigs, cows, and chickens.

Yet the potato was the most dangerous of crops. It did not keep, and it couldn't be stored from one growing season to the next. Thus every year almost two and a half million workers nearly starved in the summer when the old potatoes had all been eaten, and the new ones had not yet come in. Another reason the potato was a dangerous crop was that there was no other food to fall back on if the potato crop failed. And this is exactly what happened in 1845.

Throughout the world, one potato crop after another was killed by blight; and in October, 1845, the blight hit the potatoes in Ireland. As is the case with any hardship, the effects were not felt at once. However, six months after the disease struck, the people of Ireland were clearly starving to death. They were eating anything they could get their hands on, including diseased potatoes and food that stank because it was so rotten.

In the summer of 1846, the potato crop was poor again. The blight could not be stopped, and the people were at the end of their rope. Every rag had already been pawned to buy food. Everything that looked even faintly like food had been eaten. In October, it was reported that 7,500 people in one city were living on boiled cabbage leaves—which they ate once every forty-eight hours. In another city of 7,000 people, there was nothing at all to eat.

Children suffered most. Many had lost their voices. Many could no longer walk. Their arms seemed to have been stripped of all flesh. By April, 1847, the children looked like little old men and women of eighty years of age. Every trace of happiness had gone from their faces. Even the babies looked old.

Extremely frightened, people began to flee the country. In a great mass movement, they made their way by tens of thousands out of Ireland across the ocean to America or across the sea to England. Very few of the poor Irish who fled from Ireland during "the Great Hunger" would find riches and success in their new country. It would be their children or grandchildren who would find the way to be successful. By 1851, more than a million people had left Ireland. More than a million and a half others were dead from hunger or the fever that comes from such extremely poor living conditions. Thus in six years, the small island of Ireland was reduced from nearly nine million to six and a half million people.

Adapted from *The Great Hunger* by Cecil Woodham-Smith.
Reprinted with permission of Harper & Row © 1964.

1 **About the Reading.** If the sentence agrees with what you've just read, write *true* on the line. If the sentence disagrees, write *false* on the line.

_____ 1. Before the blight, the Irish people lived quite well.

_____ 2. Before the blight, many people in Ireland knew what it meant to be hungry.

_____ 3. Children who are starving look like very old people.

_____ 4. In order to grow potatoes, you first have to lay out a great deal of money for farm tools.

_____ 5. Most of the people who came to the United States from Ireland during the Great Hunger became rich.

_____ 6. The blight that killed the potato crop began in Ireland.

_____ 7. The effects of the blight were not felt at once.

_____ 8. The Irish people were so hungry that they would eat anything—even if it was rotten.

_____ 9. The main food of Ireland was cabbage.

_____ 10. The potato was grown because it could keep for more than a year before it rotted.

2 **More about Potatoes.** Use the words at the left to fill in the blanks. A few of the words might be new to you.

bread
brought
explored
instead
Ireland
mountains
pieces
settled
Spain
wheat
writer
1621

The potato came from South America. The first mention of the potato in a book was by a _____ in Spain in the year 1553.

More than 400 years ago, South American Indians grew potatoes high in the _____ where it was too cold for corn or _____ to grow. These people picked the potatoes, walked on them to break them into _____, and dried them in the sun. From the dried potatoes, the Indians made a light flour which they used _____ of wheat to make their _____.

The men from Spain, who _____ South America, took potatoes back to their country with them as early as 1550. From _____, potatoes were taken to Italy, then to England and France.

Potatoes were _____ into North America as early as _____. The white potato became known as the Irish potato because people from _____ brought potatoes with them when they _____ in New Hampshire in 1719.

3 **Where Would You Find It?** Choose the word that best describes where you would find the first word in the row and write it on the line to the right. Study the example before you begin.

1. **potatoes:**   trees   vines   Ireland   flowerpot   *vines*

2. **prong:**   fork   knife   spoon   soupspoon   _____

3. **the Pope:**   France   Italy   Holland   Ireland   _____

4. **menu:**   home   movies   museum   restaurant   _____

5. **champagne:**   jug   soda   bottle   bathtub   _____

6. **inmate:**   jail   attic   office   hospital   _____

7. **bellhop:**   hotel   motel   museum   restaurant   _____

8. **lipstick:**   wallet   purse   billfold   knapsack   _____

9. **keyboard:**   bar   drums   piano   restaurant   _____

10. **Amsterdam:**   Italy   Poland   Holland   Ireland   _____

11. **lobster:**   lake   ocean   river   fishbowl   _____

12. **Yankees:**   circus   museum   office   stadium   _____

13. **crosswalk:**   path   street   trail   highway   _____

14. **New Hampshire:**   West   Midwest   South   New England   _____

4 **The Ending -less.** Rewrite each word on the line to the right and add *-less* to it. Then use these words to complete the sentences below. Study the example before you begin.

hit _*hitless*_   price _____

fault _____   speech _____

sugar _____   strap _____

point _____   tree _____

1. Sandy allowed his children to chew only _____ gum.

2. The _____ diamonds on display at the museum were guarded day and night.

3. _____ bathing suits aren't seen as often at the beach this season as they were in former years.

4. The sweating hikers couldn't find any shade in which to rest on the _____ plain.

5. The pitcher pitched seven _*hitless*_ innings.

6. When Patty was informed that she had just won the grand prize of ten thousand dollars, she was _____.

7. The boss thought that Ted was the best inspector on the shift because his reports were always _____.

8. Just before Roy stormed out of the apartment, he said to his girlfriend, "It's _____ to discuss this problem any further because you're clearly out of your mind!"

Lesson 19

Digestion

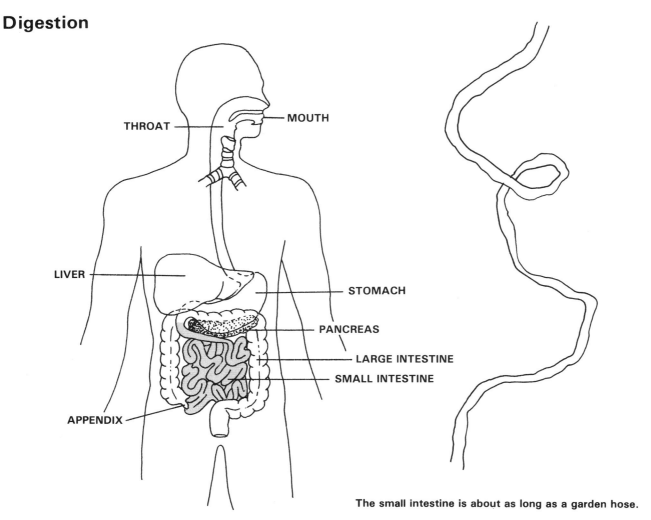

THROAT — MOUTH

LIVER

STOMACH

PANCREAS

LARGE INTESTINE

SMALL INTESTINE

APPENDIX

The small intestine is about as long as a garden hose.

Words for Study

digestion	layers	semi-liquid	bacteria
energy	greatly	intestine	poisons
worn-out	muscles	adult	murderer
tissue	digest	pancreas	husband
saliva	churned	liver	nag

Digestion

Human beings can get along without many things, but we must have air and food in order to live. Food is anything which, when taken into the body, gives energy or builds and repairs worn-out tissues. The amount of food that the human body needs depends mainly on the work it has to do. The amount of food a person should eat also depends on his health and weight. And the same person may require different amounts of food during different seasons and in different parts of the world.

Before the food we eat can be used by the body, it must be changed into liquid form. This is called the process of digestion. This entire process may take as long as eight hours.

The teeth start the work of digestion by breaking up the food into small bits. At the same time, the glands in the mouth release saliva. The saliva turns the food into a soft mass, making it easier to swallow.

The stomach, which is bag-shaped and has many layers of muscles, receives the food after it has been swallowed. The normal adult stomach can hold up to as much as 3½ pints of food. Certain glands in the stomach walls release a juice to help digest the food. Food can remain in the stomach from a few minutes to three or four hours. During this time, the food is churned by the stomach muscles. The semi-liquid mass which results from churning the food is then squeezed, a little at a time, into the small intestine.

The main work of digestion is done in the small intestine, which really isn't all that small. In an adult, this tube is about twenty feet long and one inch wide. Muscles in the wall of this tube make wave-like movements to mix the food and move it along. Glands in the walls of the small intestine release juices to help digest the food. Juices are also released by the pancreas and the liver to complete the process of digestion.

Anything that cannot be used to feed the cells of the body or repair worn-out tissues is passed into the large intestine. The large intestine stores waste until the body can get rid of it. If this process of getting rid of waste is put off for too long, millions of bacteria that live in the large intestine will attack the waste and produce poisons. Two effects of these poisons are feeling tired and feeling depressed. Far worse is the fact that these poisons are often carried to the blood. As time passes, this can lead to different kinds of diseases. For this reason, one doctor has named the large intestine, "the murderer of men."

It is very important to be relaxed when you are eating. If you eat when you are tired, angry, excited, or under stress, your food will not digest properly. Too much food eaten too fast has killed many people. One doctor said this to a wife: "If you really want to get rid of your husband, serve him a good healthy meal and then, every night, nag him while he eats it. He'll be dead in no time!"

1 **About the Reading.** Fill in the blank of each statement with the right answer.

1. A normal adult stomach can hold 3½ _____ of food.
   - (a) gallons
   - (b) ounces
   - (c) pints
   - (d) quarts

2. Most of the digestion of food takes place in the _____
   - (a) large intestine.
   - (b) pancreas.
   - (c) small intestine.
   - (d) stomach.

3. When you eat, it is important to feel _____
   - (a) angry.
   - (b) excited.
   - (c) relaxed.
   - (d) stressed.

4. The large intestine stores _____
   - (a) glands.
   - (b) hormones.
   - (c) juices.
   - (d) waste.

5. Saliva _____
   - (a) digests food.
   - (b) is a gland.
   - (c) is another word for bacteria.
   - (d) makes food soft.

6. The "murderer of men" is the _____
   - (a) heart.
   - (b) large intestine.
   - (c) liver.
   - (d) small intestine.

7. _____ is *not* important in deciding how much food a person needs to eat.
   - (a) The person's health and weight
   - (b) The work a person does
   - (c) What the person likes to eat
   - (d) Where the person lives

8. The process of digestion involves changing food from a _____

_____ state.
   (a) semi-liquid to liquid
   (b) solid to liquid
   (c) solid to semi-liquid
   (d) solid to semi-solid

9. Juices that aid digestion are released by _____
   (a) cells.
   (b) glands.
   (c) muscles.
   (d) tissues.

10. This reading is mainly about _____
   (a) how food is digested.
   (b) how important food is.
   (c) how you should feel when you eat.
   (d) the kinds of food you should eat.

2 **More about Digestion.** Put these parts of the body in the order in which they help to digest food. After you list each part in the right order, describe how it helps in the process of digestion.

Large intestine   **Small intestine**   **Stomach**   **Teeth**

1. _____

2. _____

3. _____

4. _____

3 **Cause and Effect.** Choose the effect that best matches with each cause listed below and write it on the line.

Effects:
- It passes into the large intestine.
- The body can become diseased.
- The person feels tired and upset.
- The stomach has to work harder at churning the food.

Cause	Effect
1. Not chewing food well:	_____
2. Food cannot be used by the body:	_____
3. Poisons build up in the large intestine:	_____
4. Poisons are released into the bloodstream:	_____

4 **The Human Body.** Match the words at the left with the sentence that best describes them.

glands
heart
large intestine
liver
lungs
muscles
pancreas
small intestine
spleen
stomach

_____ 1. A slang word for this part of your body is "belly."

_____ 2. These release juices that help the body in many different ways.

_____ 3. These remove carbon dioxide from the blood and give it oxygen.

_____ 4. People who drink a lot of whiskey often have trouble with this gland.

_____ 5. This is the part of the body in which digestion is completed.

_____ 6. This is the part of the body where waste is stored until the body can get rid of it.

_____ 7. This pumps blood it has received from the veins into the arteries.

_____ 8. Through contracting and relaxing, these help the body to move.

_____ 9. This is a long, soft gland which lies behind the stomach and releases juices which aid in the digestion of food.

_____ 10. This works as a blood filter and also stores blood.

5 **Word Endings.** Use the words in each group at the left to complete the sentences.

digestion
mentioned

1. Whenever Mrs. Washington _____ to her son that reading at the table was bad for his _____, he felt sick to his stomach.

agreement
moments

2. _____ after the peace _____ was signed, the two countries began to fight.

blue
continued
tissues

3. The wife _____ to buy _____ _____ for the bathroom even though her husband asked her not to.

apple
bottle
settled

4. Bucky _____ down into the armchair with a plate of cheese and crackers and a _____ of _____ juice to watch the Monday night football game.

blanket
pocket
racket

5. When Mr. Fields found he didn't have enough change in his _____ to pay the tax on the _____, his wife made such a _____ that he threw what coins he had down on the counter and stormed out of the store.

America
saliva
soda

6. Many people in _____ drink _____ in order to produce more _____ when their mouths feel dry.

handle
muscles
paddle

7. Mary could not _____ the huge _____ her brother had given her because she had no _____.

cabbage
managed
message

8. In spite of his busy day, Luke _____ to get a _____ to Ginger to pick up a head of _____ at the store for the stew he planned to make for dinner.

certain
curtains
mountain

9. Mrs. Martin was _____ she had put the _____ in with the _____ of dirty clothes that she had planned to wash and iron that afternoon.

chemicals
hospital
ideal

10. To the nurse's way of thinking, the _____ _____ would have no smell of _____ in the halls.

Lesson 20

Nail Soup

Words for Study

washtub	beggars	delicious	strength
ragged	bucket	thicken	onions
Granny	magic	several	here's
cheerfully	bacon	pocketknife	Martha

Nail Soup

A little old lady looked up from her washtub one summer day to see a stranger standing on the other side of her fence. His clothes were very ragged, but he wore them without shame.

"Good morning, Granny," the stranger said cheerfully. "Any work for a hungry young man? I always earn my dinner." With a smile and a leap, he was in the old lady's yard.

"No thanks!" she snapped. "I do my own work, and it's all been done. The wood has been chopped, the pigs are fed, and over there are the vegetables I just picked and washed. And I don't feed beggars," the old lady said firmly.

"Well, I'm no beggar, lady. If you'll just let me have a pot, I'll make my own soup."

"No one is going to tramp on my clean kitchen floor," the old lady declared, "so there's no soup pot for you."

"That's all right," he said. "Just let me use this big washtub. I'll put it back on the fire, and I'll make the best soup you ever tasted." He went to the well and got a bucket of water which he put in the pot. Then, he turned and asked, "Do you like nail soup, Granny?" He pulled a bright, shiny nail from his pocket and dropped it into the soup.

"Nail soup!" exclaimed the old woman. "I never heard of such a thing. Why, that's just a plain old carpenter's nail."

"Oh, no!" he said, winking at her. "It's a magic nail."

"Mighty thin soup, if you ask me," Granny sniffed.

"It does look thin," the young man admitted. "Maybe I put in too much water. I wish I had a ham bone. A ham bone would pep it up."

"Well," the old woman said slowly. "I have a ham bone, but it's too big for my soup pot. I'll get it for you."

While Granny was gone, the young man was busy. He took a handful of beans and a few tomatoes from the porch. Of course, Granny did not see him do this. "Here," she said as she returned from the kitchen. "I brought a few scraps of bacon, too."

"Fine! Fine! This will be delicious. Sometimes I put in a potato or two to thicken the soup, but I don't have any."

"Take some potatoes from the porch," said Granny.

The wise young stranger took several potatoes and two heads of cabbage. He chopped them up with his pocketknife and threw them into the pot. "I wonder if this nail is salty enough," he said. "It may be losing some of its strength."

"Oh, I have plenty of salt," Granny said. "I'll get it."

While she was gone, the young man quickly threw handfuls of beans, peas, and tomatoes into the pot. He had several onions in his hand when Granny came back. "I took a few onions for the soup," he said winking. "Nothing like onions for fine taste, you know."

"That's right, young man," she agreed. "Here's your salt."

The young man added salt to the pot. He peeled the onions, chopped them, and put them in. He stirred the soup and said with a wink and a smile, "Doesn't this nail soup smell good?"

"Delicious," Granny agreed.

At that moment, a neighbor was passing by. "What smells so good?" she asked.

"Martha, hurry over here," Granny yelled. "I want to show you something. This young man is making nail soup."

"Nail soup! Who ever heard of making soup with a nail!" Martha exclaimed.

"I'll get spoons and bowls," Granny said. She hurried to get them from the kitchen. Then the three of them sat down to taste the soup.

"Delicious!" said Granny.

"Delicious!" said Martha.

"Best nail soup I ever made!" said the young man.

One by one, the neighbors smelled the soup and came over. The old woman's backyard was soon filled with people, all eating nail soup. Everyone agreed that the soup was very good.

At last the big pot was empty, and the young man took out the shiny nail. He took off his hat, bowed low, and handed the nail to Granny. "A gift for you," he said smiling and winking. "Do not use it unless you have nothing else to eat. May you never go hungry."

Waving, the happy stranger leaped over the fence. He went singing down the road and was never seen again.

Adapted from the Ruth M. Harris version, *Controlled Reading Study Guide*, New York: McGraw-Hill, Inc. 1965.

1 **About the Reading.** Answer these questions.

1. What are Granny's feelings toward the young man at the beginning of the story?

2. What are Granny's feelings toward the young man at the end of the story?

3. Why do you think Granny changes the way she thinks about the young man?

4. What does the young man give Granny at the end of the story and what advice does he give her about this gift?

5. What do you think Granny does with the gift?

6. What exactly is nail soup?

7. Do you think the word *beggar* clearly describes the young man? Be sure to explain your answer.

2 **May I Take Your Order?** Read the menu and then answer the questions.

KID STUFF

A kid-size hamburger, hot dog, or grilled cheese sandwich. With a helping of french fries. And your choice of milk, chocolate milk, or soda.

Only for kids 12 and under

All for 2.09

SANDWICHES

Hamburger 1.65
Hot dog. 1.10
Fish 1.60
Shrimp salad roll 2.65
Grilled ham & cheese 1.50
Egg salad. 1.20
Peanut butter 85
Swiss cheese 1.10
Clam roll 2.40
Chicken salad. 1.85

DRINKS

Milk 60
Chocolate milk. 75
Coffee 45
Tea. 45
Iced tea (in season) 45

PLATTERS

Chopped beef platter 2.60
    No bread—just lots of beef. With french fries, tomato, and soda crackers.
Big beef platter. 2.30
    A big beef with tomato and salad dressing. Served with french fries.
Cheeseburger platter 2.45
    A great tasting sandwich served with french fries and tomato.

SIDE ORDERS

French fries. 85
Home fries 70
English muffin. 65
Toast, jelly 50
Muffin 65

DESSERTS

Cheesecake 1.50
Chocolate cake 1.25
Pie 85
    (apple, lemon, mincemeat & coconut cream)
Ice cream 75
    (2 scoops of vanilla, chocolate, or strawberry)

---

1. How much would it cost if you ordered:

_____ a. An egg salad sandwich, a cup of coffee, and a piece of coconut cream pie?

_____ b. A chopped beef platter, two glasses of milk, and a piece of chocolate cake?

_____ c. An English muffin, an order of home fries, and a cup of tea?

2. What would the waiter or waitress tell you if you ordered a glass of iced tea in December?

_____

3. What would you try to talk a young child into ordering?

_____

4. If you were really hungry, but you were trying to lose weight, what would you order?

_____

5. If you were really hungry, but you only had two dollars, what would you order?

_____

3 **Same or Opposite?** If the pair of words means the same, write *same* on the line. If the pair means the opposite, write *opposite* on the line.

1. _____ bacteria – germs

2. _____ bucket – pail

3. _____ delicious – tasty

4. _____ dangerous – harmless

5. _____ energy – pep

6. _____ faintly – barely

7. _____ fled – remained

8. _____ graceful – clumsy

9. _____ husband – wife

10. _____ nag – gripe

11. _____ overcrowded – empty

12. _____ ragged – even

13. _____ thickened – watered

14. _____ washtub – basin

15. _____ worn-out – exhausted

4 **More Work with Word Endings.** Use the words in each group at the left to complete the sentences.

million
onion

1. Jerome's eyes hurt so badly while he was peeling the _____ that he declared he'd never peel another one again—not even for a

_____ bucks!

leagues
tongue

2. The baseball manager cursed and yelled so much when anything went

wrong that he was known as having the worst _____ in both

_____ combined.

Atlantic
magic
picnic

3. Joyce and Andy went to a _____ show on the Boardwalk in

_____ City and then had a lovely _____ on the

beach.

extra vanilla	4. Louise asked the waiter if she could have an _____ scoop of _____ ice cream in her chocolate soda for no charge.
dangerous delicious	5. Martha knew it was _____ for her to be around _____ food whenever she was really trying to lose weight.
culture nature	6. Many Americans think that the way we live in our _____ destroys _____ .
broken forgotten frightened happen	7. Mark had _____ to fix the _____ lock and was _____ that a robber would just _____ to see it and break into his apartment.
disagreement payment statement	8. Mr. Herman handed the manager a written _____ in which he had explained the _____ his work crew had with the _____ they received for the job.
digest forest inquest requested	9. The doctor _____ that he be given time to _____ his dinner before going to the _____ of the corpse that the police officer had found in the _____ .
bucket faucet pocket wallet	10. When Billy turned on the _____ to fill the _____ , his _____ slipped out of his _____ .

Review: Lessons 1-20

1   **Matching.** Match each item at the left with the words that best describe it.

Group 1

artery
carbon dioxide
champagne
hormone
oxygen
saliva
swamp
vein

_____   1. A _____ is a wet piece of land.

_____   2. This carries blood away from the heart to all parts of the body.

_____   3. This carries blood from all parts of the body to the heart.

_____   4. This is a juice in the mouth that helps to turn food from a solid to a semi-liquid form.

_____   5. This is formed in one part of the body and carried by the bloodstream to another part to do a certain job.

_____   6. This is often served at weddings or fancy parties.

_____   7. This is what we exhale when we breathe.

_____   8. This is what we inhale when we breathe.

Group 2

Thomas Edison
Fourth of July
Huron
New England
North Pole
Pearl Harbor
Pueblo
Yankees

_____   1. This is a term used to describe people living in the North during the War Between the States; it is also the name of a baseball team in the American League.

_____   2. He invented the light bulb.

_____   3. Japan bombed this place on December 7, 1941.

_____   4. New Hampshire is in this part of the United States.

_____   5. This is one of the five Great Lakes in the United States.

_____   6. This holiday started when the United States declared its freedom from England.

_____   7. This is the name of an Indian people who live in the American Southwest.

_____   8. This is where little children think Santa Claus lives.

Group 3

A.M.
B.C.
Dr.
etc.
Mrs.
Ms.
P.M.
TV

_____ 1. a woman who is either married or single

_____ 2. a woman who is married

_____ 3. and so forth

_____ 4. after noon

_____ 5. before noon

_____ 6. doctor

_____ 7. the time before the birth of Jesus

_____ 8. what people often watch to relax or because they have nothing better to do

2 **Word Study.** Choose the right answer from the four choices and write it on the line.

_____ 1. What do you find in most rowboats?
(a) machines   (b) oars   (c) paddles   (d) prongs

_____ 2. Which of these animals is noted for moving slowly?
(a) camel   (b) cattle   (c) turkey   (d) turtle

_____ 3. Which of these countries is a group of islands?
(a) Germany   (b) Italy   (c) Japan   (d) Poland

_____ 4. In which of these sports do the players ride horses?
(a) handball   (b) polo   (c) tennis   (d) track and field

_____ 5. During the lesson on digestion, the teacher drew _____ on the blackboard so the students could better understand this process.
(a) concepts   (b) diagrams   (c) ideals   (d) traits

_____ 6. When a mouse is caught by a cat, hormones are _____ by glands in the mouse to help bring about a painless death.
(a) received   (b) reflected   (c) regarded   (d) released

_____ 7. Before Holly lit her cigarette, she asked, "Do you _____ to my smoking in your office?"
(a) affect   (b) collect   (c) object   (d) respect

_____ 8. A word that describes most fish is _____.
(a) scaly   (b) scratchy   (c) sneaky   (d) spongy

_____ 9. Who displayed a lot of energy when it came to eating?
(a) Diamond Jim Brady   (c) Thomas A. Edison
(b) Babe Ruth   (d) Adolf Hitler

_____ 10. Where is the country of Egypt located?
     (a) Africa   (b) Asia   (c) North America   (d) South America

_____ 11. Who is well-known for a huge belly?
     (a) Black Beauty   (c) Pinocchio
     (b) Cinderella   (d) Santa Claus

_____ 12. Which word best describes the feelings of a person who always
     seems to be happy one minute and depressed the next?
     (a) easiness   (b) kindness   (c) laziness   (d) moodiness

_____ 13. The Earth is an example of a _____.
     (a) disc   (b) meteor   (c) planet   (d) star

_____ 14. Which word has to do with the ideas, traits, and skills of a group
     of people?
     (a) culture   (b) ideals   (c) make-believe   (d) nature

3   **Which Word Does Not Fit?** Choose the word in each line that does not fit with
the rest and write it on the line to the right.

1. diner	drugstore	laundromat	sidewalk	_____
2. common	normal	rare	widespread	_____
3. bookworm	dunce	egghead	student	_____
4. cattle	cowboy	Midwest	range	_____
5. intestines	nostrils	saliva	stomach	_____
6. Baltimore	Boston	Detroit	El Dorado	_____
7. combine	join	merge	split	_____
8. cut	pocketknife	rip	tear	_____
9. answer	mention	reply	respond	_____
10. channel	newscast	newspaper	*TV Guide*	_____
11. butterfly	fly	grasshopper	turtle	_____
12. dirty	greasy	messy	silky	_____
13. meteor	meteorite	planet	sun	_____
14. field	meadow	skyscraper	wilderness	_____
15. clam	lobster	oyster	roast beef	_____

4   **Four-letter Words.** Use the words at the left to complete the sentences.

acre
Asia
busy
disc
hero
item
menu
mitt
Ohio
soda
toes
view

1. Flying saucers are in the shape of a _____ according to people who have seen them.

2. Babe Ruth was a _____ to millions of American baseball fans.

3. Walter read an _____ in the newspaper about a judge who sentenced a man to more than 900 years in jail because he threatened to shoot a corpse.

4. Mike's _____ felt completely frozen by the time the football game was over.

5. Granny's dream was to own an _____ of land so she could build her very own house.

6. William's family moved from _____ to New Hampshire when he was seven years old.

7. Many people in _____ depend upon camels the way Americans depend upon automobiles and trucks.

8. Mr. West ordered champagne for his wife Martha and a bottle of _____ for himself.

9. The boss was too _____ to see Bart just then, so the two men agreed to go over the plans for the new machine that afternoon.

10. The catcher threw down his _____ in disgust when he let the pitch get by him.

11. The _____ from the bridge was so beautiful that Ginger wished she could just stay there and never return to the city.

12. The waitress printed the day's _____ on a blackboard behind the counter.

5   **Syllables.** Each of these words has more than one syllable. Write the syllables on the lines to the right of each word.

1. childhood   _____ • _____

2. wonderful   _____ • _____ • _____

3. tissue   _____ • _____

4. narrowly   _____ • _____ • _____

5. delightful   _____ • _____ • _____

6. hardship   _____ • _____

7. respectful   _____ • _____ • _____

8. nervously   _____ • _____ • _____

9. champagne   _____ • _____

10. midmorning   _____ • _____ • _____

Word Index: Lessons 1-20

A
accept
accident
acre
action
Adolf
adult
affect
Africa
agreement
airplane
Al
A.M.
America
American
among
amount
Amsterdam
anyone
apple
artery
Asia
aside
Atlantic
Atlantic City
atmosphere
attack
attic
aware
awfully
ax(e)

B
Babe
backyard
bacon
bacteria
bagful
baggage
baggy
balloon
Baltimore
Bambino
bartender
basement
battery
battleground
battleship
beam
beeline
beggar
beginning
belief
believer
bellhop
belly
belonging

beneath
berry
bicycle
bidder
bidding
billionth
birdhouse
blanket
blender
blight
blindness
bodily
boring
borrow
bottle
bottom
boxcar
boxing
Brady
brandy
breadboard
breather
breezy
broiler
brotherhood
bubble
bucket
built
bully
bunny
bushy
butterfly
buzzer

C
cabbage
camel
campground
carbon
carbon dioxide
cargo
Carver, G.W.
carving
cattle
caveman
champagne
channel
chat
cheerfully
cheeseburger
chemical
childhood
choosy
choppy
Christmas Eve
churn
clammy

clearly
cloudburst
clubhouse
clumsily
clumsy
coating
collect
collector
color
colorful
coloring
comedown
concept
condition
conduct
conductor
connect
continue
cooky
corn bread
countdown
county
crab
cranberry
creamy
crisp
crossing
crudely
culture
curdle
curly
customer

D
dangerous
daring
dashboard
deaf
deafness
dealer
degree
delicious
delightful
depress
desert
despite
detail
diagram
dial
diamond
diary
differently
digest
digestion
digger
dining
disagreement

disc
disease
dishwasher
distress
dogwood
downward
dozen
drawing
drummer
duckpin
dusty
dying

E
easily
easiness
eater
Edison, T.
effect
energy
entire
entirely
escape
exhale

F
faintly
farewell
fatty
faultless
feeler
fever
fishbowl
fled
flee
flicker
flint
flipper
floorboard
floppy
flowery
foolish
foolishly
forest
foxhole
Frank
frank
freeborn
freeform
freeload
freely
friendship
full-grown
fully

G
gearshift
German

Germany
god
good-looking
graceful
grandchildren
Granny
grasshopper
gravy
greasy
greatly
greedily
greenhouse
growth
gummy
gunner

H
hailstone
half-hour
hamburger
handball
handcuff
handicap
handle
handlebar
handpick
handshake
handsome
harbor
hardship
Hawaii
heap
hearing
heaven
here's
Herman
hero
high-priced
high-rise
hiker
history
Hitler, A.
hitless
holiday
Holland
hooker
hormone
hospital
hot dog
hothouse
hump
humpbacked
hunger
hungry
Huron
husband

I
ideal
ill-mannered
immense
inch
Indian
inmate
inning
insider
inspect
inspector
intermission
intenstine
invader
invention
inventor
Ireland
Irish
island
Italy
item
itself

J
jackhammer
jackknife
jackpot
James
Japan
jewelry
Jewish
jog
jogger
jogging
Johnson
jumper

K
killer
kindhearted
kindness

L
ladybug
lash
latch
layer
laziness
leafy
league
learner
lefthanded
lightly
likely
liner
line-up
liver
lob
lobster

locate
locker
logger
loneliness
lying

M
ma'am
magic
make-believe
manners
Martha
matting
M.D.
meadow
medicine
menu
merging
message
meteor
meteorite
Michigan
midmorning
Midwest
milkshake
mining
misfit
monkeyshines
moodiness
moody
moonlight
moonshine
mostly
mound
mountain
mousetrap
mousy
mouthpart
movement
muffin
muggy
murderer
muscle
museum
mustn't

N
nag
narrow
narrowly

nature
nervously
nervy
nevertheless
New Hampshire
newscast
newsletter
newsreel
New York City
normal
normally
North America
North Pole
nostril

O
object
offer
office
officer
Ohio
one-fourth
one-third
onion
opium
orange
outhouse
outline
outsider
overcrowd
overhanging
overheard
overload
overturn
oxen
oxygen
oyster

P
pacemaker
paddle
padlock
pancreas
panty
pasty
patter
pattern
pearl
Pearl Harbor
peppy
per

perform
performer
perhaps
Peter
picnic
piggyback
pigtail
pipeline
planet
pleasing
plural
P.M.
pocket
pocketknife
pointless
poison
Poland
pollen
polo
potty
prayer
pretend
priceless
printer
process
produce
program
prompt
promptly
prong
protect
prove
Pueblo

Q

R
racket
radio
ragged
railway
rainstorm
ray
reader
receive
reflect
regard
release
respectful
restaurant
result

rewrite
rigging
righthanded
runner
rusty

S
salad
saliva
sandpaper
sandy
Santa Claus
scaly
scary
screwdriver
selfish
semi-liquid
setting
settle
several
shaggy
shaker
shameful
sheepskin
shortcut
shred
shrub
silky
singular
sisterhood
skipper
skylight
skyline
skyscraper
slop
sloppy
smoggy
snakebite
snapper
soapy
soda
soupspoon
South America
southpaw
South Pole
southwest
sox
spade
speechless
speedily

speedy
spelling
spider
spongy
squish
stadium
stank
starfish
statement
steal
steer
step-by-step
stomach
stomp
strainer
strapless
strawberry
strength
strictly
string bean
stroll
student
stupid
sudden
suddenly
suffer
sunflower
sunset
sunstroke
suntan
swallow
swamp
swirl

T
tearful
tennis
tenpin
termite
terrible
Texas
therefore
they've
thicken
Thomas
thunder
tiny
tissue
toe
Tommy

tongue
topping
total
trader
training
trait
treeless
truly
tuner
turkey
turtle
TV

U
unaware
uncommon
unluckily
upper
upward
used

V
vegetable
vein
view

W
waitress
washer
washtub
watcher
wheezy
whiskey
widely
wilderness
wince
wind
wiper
wishful
wonderful
World War II
worn-out
worry
worship

X

Y
Yankee
yellow

Z

Word Index: Books 1-4

a
able
about
above
accept
accident
according
ace
acre
across
act
action
actor
ad
add
admit
Adolf
adult
advice
affect
afford
afraid
Africa
after
afternoon
afterward
again
against
age
ago
agree
agreement
ahead
ahoy
aid
ail
aim
air
airplane
Al
alarm
alive
all
allow
all right
all-star
almost
alone
along
alphabet
already
also
although
always
am
A.M.
America

American
among
amount
Amsterdam
amuse
amusement
an
and
Andy
anger
angry
animal
Ann(e)
another
answer
ant
any
anybody
anymore
anyone
anything
anyway
anywhere
apart
apartment
ape
apple
April
are
aren't
arm
armchair
armful
army
around
arrive
art
artery
as
ash
ashtray
Asia
aside
ask
asleep
at
ate
Atlantic
Atlantic City
atmosphere
attack
attic
August
aunt
auto
automobile
autumn

avoid
awake
aware
away
awful
awfully
awoke
ax(e)
babe
baby
babysit
babysitter
back
backbone
backfire
background
backpack
backrest
backside
backtrack
backwoods
backyard
bacon
bacteria
bad
badge
badly
bag
bagful
baggage
baggy
bail
bait
bake
baker
bald
ball
balloon
Baltimore
Bambino
band
bang
bank
banker
banner
bar
barbed
barber
bare
barely
barge
bark
barn
Bart
bartender
base
baseball

basement
basin
basket
basketball
bat
batch
bath
bathe
bathing
bathroom
bathtub
batter
battery
battle
battleground
battleship
B.C.
be
beach
bead
beam
bean
bear
beard
beast
beat
beaten
beautiful
beauty
became
because
become
bed
bedding
bedroom
bedspread
bedtime
bee
beef
beeline
been
beep
beer
beet
before
beg
began
beggar
begin
beginner
beginning
begun
behave
behind
belief
believe
believer

bell
bellhop
belly
belong
belonging
below
belt
Ben
bench
bend
bender
beneath
bent
berry
berserk
beside
besides
best
bet
better
between
bib
Bible
bicycle
bid
bidder
bidding
big
bigwig
bike
bill
billfold
billion
billionth
Billy
bin
bind
binge
bingo
birch
bird
birdhouse
birth
birthday
bit
bitch
bite
bitten
bitter
black
blackbird
blackboard
blackmail
blacksmith
blacktop
blade
blame

blank
blanket
blast
bleach
bleed
blend
blender
bless
blessing
blew
blight
blind
blindly
blindness
blink
blob
block
blood
bloodstream
bloody
bloom
blouse
blow
blowout
blown
blue
blues
bluff
blurt
blush
board
boarder
boardwalk
boast
boat
Bob
Bobby
bobsled
bodily
body
bodyguard
boil
boiler
bold
bolt
bomb
bond
bone
bony
book
bookcase
bookmark
bookshelf
bookstore
bookworm
boom
boot

booth
booty
booze
bop
border
bore
boring
born
borrow
boss
bossy
Boston
both
bottle
bottom
bought
bounce
bouncer
bouncy
bound
bow
bowl
bowling
box
boxcar
boxer
boxing
boy
Boy Scout
brace
bracelet
Brady
brag
braid
brain
brainy
brake
branch
brand
brand-new
brandy
brave
bravely
bread
breadboard
break
breakdown
breakfast
breakthrough
breast
breath
breathe
breather
breathing
breathless
breed
breeze

breezy
brew
bribe
brick
bride
bridge
bright
brightly
bring
brink
broil
broiler
broke
broken
brook
broom
brother
brotherhood
brotherly
brought
brown
brownie
bruise
brush
bubble
buck
bucket
Bucky
bud
buddy
bug
buggy
build
building
built
bulb
bulk
bulky
bull
bully
bum
bump
bumper
bumpy
bun
bunch
bunk
bunny
bunt
burn
burner
burp
burst
bus
bush
bushy
busily

business
bust
busy
busybody
but
butch
butter
butterfly
buy
buzz
buzzer
by
cab
cabbage
cage
cake
California
call
calm
calmly
came
camel
camp
camper
campground
camping
can
cancer
candy
cane
cannot
can't
cap
cape
Cape Cod
car
carbon
carbon dioxide
card
cardboard
care
careful
careless
cargo
carpenter
carpet
carry
cart
carve
Carver, G.W.
carving
case
cash
cast
cat
catbird
catcall

catch
catcher
catfish
cattle
catty
caught
cause
caution
cautious
cave
caveman
ceiling
celebrate
cell
cellar
cent
center
certain
certainly
chain
chair
chalk
chalkboard
champagne
chance
change
channel
charge
Charles
charm
chart
chase
chat
cheap
cheaply
cheapskate
cheat
check
checkbook
checkers
cheek
cheer
cheerful
cheerfully
Cheerios
cheerleader
cheery
cheese
cheeseburger
cheesecake
chemical
chess
chessboard
chest
chestnut
chew
chick

chicken
child
childhood
children
chill
chilly
chin
chip
chirp
chocolate
choice
choke
choose
choosy
chop
choppy
chopstick
chore
chose
chosen
chow
Christ
Christian
Christmas
Christmas Eve
chrome
chunk
church
churn
cider
cigar
cigarette
cinch
cinder
Cinderella
circle
circus
city
claim
clam
clammy
clap
Clark
clash
class
classroom
claw
clay
clean
cleaner
clear
clearing
clearly
clench
clerk
click
cliff

climb
clip
clippers
clipping
clock
close
cloth
clothes
clothesline
clothespin
clothing
cloud
cloudburst
cloudless
cloudy
clown
club
clubhouse
clue
clumsily
clumsy
clung
clutch
clutter
coach
coal
coast
coaster
coat
coating
cob
cobweb
cock
cockroach
cocky
cocoa
coconut
cod
code
coffee
coffeecake
coil
coin
coke
cold
cold-blooded
collect
collector
color
coloring
colt
comb
combine
come
comeback
comedown
comfort

coming
command
commander
commandment
comment
commit
common
commonly
compare
compete
complain
complaint
complete
completely
complex
comply
compose
composed
composer
compound
compute
computer
conceal
concern
concert
concept
conclude
condition
conduct
conductor
cone
confess
confide
confine
conform
confront
confuse
connect
consent
consonant
construct
consume
consumer
contain
container
content
continue
contract
control
convict
convince
cook
cookbook
cooky
cool
cop
cope

copper
copy
copycat
cord
cork
corn
corn bread
corner
cornstarch
corny
corpse
cost
costly
cot
couch
cough
could
couldn't
count
countdown
counter
countless
country
countrymen
county
course
court
courthouse
courtroom
cousin
cove
cover
covering
cow
cowboy
crab
crack
cracker
cramp
cranberry
crane
crash
crate
crawl
crazy
cream
creamy
creep
creepy
crew
crib
crime
crisp
crook
crooked
crop
cross

crossing	Dave	die	doormat	duckpin	English	fair
crosswalk	dawn	difference	doorway	due	enjoy	fairly
crouch	day	different	dope	dues	enough	fairness
crow	daybreak	differently	dose	dug	enter	fairy
crowbar	daydream	dig	dot	duke	entire	faith
crowd	dead	digest	double	dull	entirely	faithful
crown	deadline	digestion	dough	dumb	escape	fake
crude	deadly	digger	doughnut	dummy	etc.	fall
crudely	deaf	dill	down	dump	eve	fallen
cruise	deafness	dim	downfall	dunce	even	false
cruiser	deal	dime	downhearted	dune	evening	fame
crumb	dealer	dine	downhill	dunk	ever	family
crunch	dear	diner	downpour	during	every	fan
crush	death	dining	downright	dusk	everybody	fancy
crust	debate	dinner	downstairs	dust	everyone	fang
crutch	decay	dip	downstream	dusty	everything	far
cry	December	dipper	down-to-earth	Dutch	everywhere	fare
crybaby	decide	dipstick	downtown	dying	exact	farewell
cub	deck	dirt	downward	each	exactly	farm
cube	declare	dirty	doze	ear	example	farmer
cud	deed	disagree	dozen	early	exceed	farmhouse
cuff	deep	disagreement	Dr.	earn	except	farther
culture	deer	disc	drag	earring	exchange	fast
cup	defeat	discharge	drain	earth	excite	fat
cupboard	defend	discover	drank	easily	exclaim	fate
cupcake	define	discovery	drape	easiness	exclude	father
cupful	deflate	discuss	draw	east	excuse	fatty
curb	degree	disease	drawing	Easter	exercise	faucet
curdle	delicious	disgust	drawn	easy	exert	fault
cure	delight	dish	dread	eat	exhale	faultless
curl	delightful	dishpan	dreadful	eaten	exhaust	faulty
curly	demand	dishrag	dream	eater	exist	fear
curse	den	dishtowel	dreamer	Eddie	expand	feast
curtain	Dennis	dishwasher	dreamland	edge	expect	feather
curve	dense	dishwater	drench	edgy	expel	February
customer	dent	display	dress	Edison, T.	expense	fed
cut	dentist	dispose	dresser	eel	expert	fee
cute	depend	distress	dressing	effect	explain	feed
cutters	depress	disturb	drew	egg	explode	feel
cutting	describe	ditch	drift	egghead	explore	feeler
dab	desert	dive	drill	eggshell	explorer	feeling
dad	deserve	diver	drink	Egypt	expose	feet
daddy	desire	do	drip	eight	express	fell
daily	desk	dock	drive	eighteen	ex-slave	felt
dam	despite	doctor	driven	eighth	extend	female
damp	dessert	dodge	driver	eighty	extent	fence
Dan	destroy	does	driveway	either	extra	fetch
dance	detach	doesn't	drone	elbow	extreme	fever
dancer	detail	dog	drop	El Dorado	extremely	few
danger	Detroit	doggy	drove	eleven	eye	fib
dangerous	devote	dogwood	drown	elf	eyesight	fiddle
dare	diagram	dollar	drug	elk	eyestrain	fiddler
daring	dial	dome	drugstore	elm	face	field
dark	diamond	done	drum	else	fact	fifteen
darn	diary	donkey	drummer	employer	factor	fifty
dart	dice	don't	drumstick	empty	fad	fig
dash	Dick	door	drunk	end	fade	fight
dashboard	did	doorbell	dry	ending	fail	fighter
date	diddle	doorknob	dryer	energy	faint	figure
daughter	didn't	doorman	duck	England	faintly	file

fill	flush	fresh	gift	grand	gut	haven't
film	flute	freshly	gill	grandchildren	gutter	Hawaii
filter	fly	freshman	gin	grandfather	guy	hay
fin	fog	Friday	Ginger	grandmother	had	he
find	foggy	friend	gingerbread	granny	hadn't	head
fine	foil	friendly	girl	grape	hail	heading
finger	fold	friendship	girlfriend	grapefruit	hailstone	headquarters
fingernail	folder	fright	give	grass	hair	health
fingerprint	folk	frighten	given	grasshopper	hairbrush	healthy
fir	folks	frog	glad	grave	haircut	heap
fire	fond	from	glance	graveyard	hairless	hear
firecracker	food	front	gland	gravy	hairpin	heard
firelight	fool	froze	glare	gray	hairy	hearing
fireplace	foolish	frozen	glass	grease	half	heart
firetrap	foolishly	fruit	gleam	greasy	half-hour	heartbeat
firm	foot	fruitcake	glitter	great	hall	heartbreak
firmly	football	fry	globe	greatly	halt	heat
first	footprint	fudge	gloom	Greece	ham	heater
fish	for	full	gloomy	greed	hamburger	heaven
fishbowl	forbid	full-grown	glove	greedily	hammer	heavy
fisherman	force	fully	glow	greedy	hand	heck
fist	forefeet	fume	glue	Greek	handball	he'd
fit	forest	fun	gnarled	green	handbag	heel
fitting	forge	fund	gnash	greenhouse	handcuff	height
five	forget	funk	gnat	greens	handful	held
fix	forgetful	funny	gnaw	greet	handicap	helicopter
flag	forgive	fur	gnawing	grew	handle	hell
flake	forgiven	further	gnome	grill	handlebar	he'll
flaky	forgot	fuse	go	grin	handpick	hello
flame	forgotten	fuss	goal	grind	handshake	help
flap	fork	fussy	gob	grip	handsome	helper
flare	form	gag	gobble	gripe	handwriting	helpful
flash	forth	Gail	God	grown	handy	helpless
flashlight	forty	gain	god	groom	hang	hem
flat	forty-niner	gale	godmother	grouch	hanger	hen
flea	forward	gall	goes	grouchy	hangover	her
fled	fought	galley	gold	ground	happen	herb
flee	found	gallon	golden	group	happily	Herb
fleet	four	game	gold-plated	grow	happiness	herd
flesh	fourteen	gang	golly	growl	happy	here
flew	fourth	garbage	gone	grown	harbor	here's
flicker	Fourth of July	gas	gong	grownup	hard	Herman
flight	fox	gate	goo	growth	hardly	hero
flint	foxhole	gauze	good	grudge	hardship	herself
flip	frame	gave	good-looking	guard	hardware	he's
flipper	France	gaze	goodness	guess	harm	hey
flirt	frank	gear	goods	guest	harmful	hi
float	Frank	gearshift	goof	guide	harmless	hid
flock	freak	gee	goofy	guilt	harp	hidden
flood	free	geese	goose	guilty	harsh	hide
floor	freeborn	gem	gorge	gulf	Harvey	hide-and-seek
floorboard	freedom	gent	gosh	gull	has	hideout
flop	freeform	gentle	got	gully	hasn't	high
floppy	freeload	gentleman	gotten	gulp	hat	high-class
flour	freely	gently	gown	gum	hatch	highness
flow	freeway	George	grab	gumdrop	hate	high-priced
flower	freeze	germ	grace	gummy	hall	high-rise
flowerpot	freezer	German	graceful	gun	haunt	high school
flowery	freight	Germany	grade	gunner	haunted	highway
flu	French	get	grain	gust	have	hike

hiker	house	infield	James	kid	late	lightly
hill	household	inflate	January	kidnap	lately	like
him	housewife	inform	Japan	kill	later	likely
himself	housework	inhale	jar	killer	laugh	limb
hind	how	injure	jaw	kin	laughter	lime
hint	however	injury	jazz	kind	laundromat	limit
hip	how's	ink	jeans	kindhearted	laundry	limp
hire	hug	inland	jeep	kindness	law	Linda
his	huge	inmate	jeer	kinfolk	lawful	line
hiss	huh	inning	Jello	king	lawn	liner
history	hum	inquest	jelly	Kirk	lawyer	lining
hit	human	inquire	jerk	kiss	lay	line-up
Hitler, A.	hump	insect	Jerome	kit	layer	link
hitless	humpbacked	inside	Jesus	kitchen	laziness	lint
hitter	hunch	insider	jet	kite	lazy	lip
hive	hundred	insight	Jew	kitty	lead	lipstick
hobby	hung	insist	jewelry	knack	leader	liquid
hock	hunger	inspect	Jewish	knapsack	leaf	list
hoist	hungry	inspector	Jill	knee	leafy	listen
hold	hunt	inspire	Jim	knee-cap	league	lit
holder	hunter	instead	Joan	knee-deep	leak	little
holdup	hurl	instruct	job	kneel	leaky	live
hole	Huron	intend	jobless	knelt	lean	lively
holiday	hurry	intense	jog	knew	leap	liver
Holland	hurt	intent	jogger	knickknack	leapfrog	living
Holly	husband	intermission	jogging	knife	learn	load
home	hush	intestine	John	knight	learner	loaf
homebody	hut	into	Johnson	knit	leash	loan
homeland	I	invade	join	knob	least	lob
homeless	ice	invader	joint	knock	leather	lobby
homemade	ice cream	invent	joke	knockout	leave	lobster
home run	icing	invention	joker	knot	led	locate
homesick	icy	inventor	Jones	knotty	ledge	lock
homework	I'd	invite	jot	know	Lee	locker
homey	idea	involve	joy	known	left	lodge
honey	ideal	IOU	Joyce	lab	lefthanded	log
honeybee	if	Ireland	joyful	lace	leg	logger
honk	ill	Irish	judge	lack	lemon	lone
honor	ill-mannered	iron	jug	lacy	lend	loneliness
hood	I'll	is	juice	lady	lent	lonely
hook	I'm	island	juicy	ladybug	Lent	long
hooker	immense	isn't	July	lake	less	longing
hop	import	it	jump	laid	lesson	look
hope	important	Italy	jumper	lamb	let	loose
hopeful	imported	itch	jumpy	lame	let's	loosen
hopeless	impose	item	June	lamp	letter	lord
hormone	impress	its	junk	lance	library	lose
horn	improper	it's	jury	land	lice	loss
horse	improperly	itself	just	landlady	lick	lost
horseback	improve	I've	jut	landlord	lid	lot
horseplay	impure	ivy	Kate	landmark	lie	loud
hose	in	jab	keel	landowner	life	loudly
hospital	inch	jack	keep	lane	lifeboat	Louise
hot	include	Jack	keeper	lap	lifeguard	lousy
hot dog	income	jacket	keg	lard	lifetime	love
hotel	increase	jackhammer	kept	large	lift	lovely
hothouse	index	jackknife	ketchup	lark	light	lover
hour	Indian	jackpot	key	lash	lighten	low
hourglass	indoors	jail	keyboard	last	lighter	lowdown
hourly	infect	jam	kick	latch	lighthouse	lower

loyal
loyally
loyalty
luck
luckily
lucky
lug
Luke
lukewarm
lump
lunch
lung
lunge
lurch
lying
ma'am
machine
Mack
mad
made
madly
magic
maid
mail
mailbox
mailman
main
mainly
make
make-believe
maker
male
mall
malt
mammal
man
manager
mankind
manner
manners
Mansfield
many
map
march
March
mark
Mark
marry
Martha
Martin
Mary
mash
mask
mass
mat
match
matchbook
mate
math
matter

Matthew
matting
may
May
maybe
Mayflower
M.D.
me
meadow
meal
mealtime
mean
meaning
meant
meat
meatball
meatless
medicine
meet
meeting
melt
men
mend
mention
menu
merge
merging
mess
message
messy
met
meteor
meteorite
mice
Michigan
middle
middle-aged
midmorning
midnight
Midwest
might
mighty
Mike
mild
mildly
mile
milk
milkshake
million
mince
mincemeat
mind
mine
miner
mining
mint
minute
mirror
miscount
misfit

misjudge
misplace
miss
misspell
mist
mistake
mistaken
mistreat
mistrust
mitt
mix
moan
mob
mock
moist
moisten
mold
moldy
mom
moment
mommy
Monday
money
monkey
monkeyshines
month
mood
moodiness
moody
moon
moonlight
moonshine
moose
mop
mope
more
morning
most
mostly
motel
mother
mound
mountain
mouse
mousetrap
mousy
mouth
mouthful
mouthpart
move
movement
movie
mow
mower
Mr.
Mrs.
Ms.
much
mud
muddy

muffin
mug
mugger
muggy
mule
munch
murder
murderer
murmur
muscle
muse
museum
must
mustn't
mute
my
myself
nag
nail
name
nap
narrow
narrowly
nasty
nature
naughty
near
nearby
nearly
neat
neatly
neck
necktie
nectar
need
needless
needy
neighbor
neighborhood
neither
nerve
nervous
nervously
nervy
nest
net
never
nevertheless
new
newcomer
New England
New Hampshire
news
newscast
newsletter
newspaper
newsreel
newsstand
New Year's Day
New Year's Eve

New York
New York City
next
nice
nick
nickname
night
nightclub
nine
nineteen
ninety
nip
no
nobody
nod
noise
noisily
noisy
none
nonsense
nook
noon
no one
noose
nope
nor
normal
normally
north
North America
North Pole
Norway
nose
nostril
nosy
not
notch
note
notebook
nothing
notice
November
now
nowhere
nude
nudge
numb
number
nurse
nut
nutty
oak
oar
oat
oatmeal
object
ocean
o'clock
October
odd

oddly
of
off
offer
office
officer
often
oh
Ohio
oil
okay
old
on
once
one
one-celled
one-fourth
one-half
one-third
only
onion
onto
ooze
open
opium
opposite
or
orange
order
other
ouch
ought
ounce
our
ours
ourselves
out
outcome
outdoors
outer
outfield
outhouse
outline
outlook
outnumber
outside
outsider
outskirts
outsmart
outstanding
oven
over
overall
overalls
overboard
overcoat
overcome
overcrowd
overdone
overdraw

overflow
overgrown
overhanging
overhead
overheard
overload
overlook
overnight
overseas
overtime
overturn
overweight
owe
own
owner
ox
oxen
oxygen
oyster
pace
pacemaker
pack
pact
pad
padding
paddle
padlock
page
paid
pail
pain
painful
painless
paint
paintbrush
painter
painting
pair
pale
palm
pan
pancake
pancreas
pane
pant
pants
panty
paper
park
part
party
pass
passbook
Passover
passport
password
past
paste
pasty
pat

patch
path
patter
pattern
patty
Paul
pause
pave
paving
paw
pawn
pay
paycheck
payday
payment
pea
peace
peaceful
peacefully
peach
peanut
pear
pearl
Pearl Harbor
peck
peek
peel
peeler
peep
peer
pen
penny
people
pep
pepper
peppy
per
perch
perform
performer
perhaps
period
perk
person
pest
pet
Peter
phone
phony
piano
pick
pickle
picnic
picture
pie
piece
pig
piggy
piggyback
pigpen

pigtail
pile
pill
pillow
pin
pinch
pine
Ping-Pong
pink
Pinocchio
pint
pipe
pipeline
pit
pitch
pitcher
pitchfork
pity
place
plain
plainly
plan
plane
planet
plant
plate
platter
play
player
playground
plea
plead
pleasant
please
pleased
pleasing
pledge
plenty
plot
plow
plug
plum
plump
plunge
plural
plus
P.M.
poach
pocket
pocketknife
pod
point
pointless
poison
poke
poker
Poland
pole
police
policeman

pollen
polo
pond
pool
poor
poorhouse
poorly
pop
popcorn
Pope
porch
pork
port
pot
potato
potato chip
potty
pouch
pounce
pound
pour
pout
practice
praise
prance
pray
prayer
preach
preacher
present
president
press
pretend
pretty
pretzel
price
priceless
pride
prince
print
printer
prize
probably
problem
process
produce
program
prompt
promptly
prong
proof
prop
proper
properly
property
protect
proud
proudly
prove
prune

pry
pub
Pueblo
puff
puffy
pull
pulse
pump
punch
punk
punt
purr
purse
push
put
putty
quack
quart
quarter
quarterback
queen
queer
question
quick
quickly
quiet
quit
quite
quote
race
rack
racket
radio
raft
rag
rage
ragged
raid
rail
railroad
railway
rain
rainbow
raincoat
rainstorm
rainy
raise
rake
ram
ramp
ran
rang
range
rank
rare
rarely
rash
rat
rate
raw

ray
reach
react
read
reader
reading
ready
real
really
rear
reason
recall
receive
recipe
record
recover
recovery
red
reduce
reel
reflect
reform
refresh
refrigerator
refund
refuse
regard
reject
rejection
rejoice
relate
relax
release
remain
remains
remark
remember
remind
remove
renew
rent
repaid
repair
repeat
reply
report
reporter
request
require
respect
respectful
respond
rest
restaurant
restless
restroom
result
retire
retreat
return

reveal
revive
rewrite
rhyme
rib
rice
rich
rid
ridden
ride
ridge
rig
rigging
right
righthanded
rim
ring
ringside
rinse
rip
ripe
rise
risen
risk
risky
river
road
roadwork
roar
roast
rob
robber
robbery
robe
rock
rocky
rod
rode
role
roll
roller
Rome
roof
room
rope
rose
rosebud
rosy
rot
rotten
rough
round
route
row
rowboat
Roy
royal
royally
royalty
rub

rubber
rude
rug
rule
ruler
run
rung
runner
runny
runt
rush
rust
rusty
rut
Ruth
sack
sad
sadly
sadness
safe
safely
said
sail
sailor
sake
salad
sale
salesman
saliva
salt
salty
Sam
same
sample
sand
sandpaper
sandwich
sandy
sang
sank
Santa Claus
sat
Saturday
sauce
saucepan
saucer
save
savings
saw
say
saying
says
scald
scale
scaly
scar
scare
scarecrow
scarf
scary

scheme
school
scold
scoop
scorch
score
scoreboard
scotch
Scotch
Scott
scour
scout
scram
scrap
scrape
scraper
scratch
scratchy
scream
screech
screen
screw
screwdriver
scribe
script
scroll
scrounge
scrub
scruff
sea
seacoast
seafood
seal
seaport
search
season
seat
seaweed
second
see
seed
seek
seem
seen
seep
self
selfish
sell
semi-
send
sense
sent
sentence
September
serve
set
setting
settle
seven
seventeen

seventh
seventy
several
sex
shack
shade
shady
shaggy
shake
shaken
shaker
shaky
shame
shameful
shape
share
shark
sharp
sharply
shatter
shave
she
she'd
sheep
sheepskin
sheer
sheet
shelf
shell
shelter
she's
shift
shine
shiny
ship
shipwreck
shirt
shock
shook
shoot
shop
shopper
shopping
shore
short
shortcake
shortcut
shorts
shortstop
shot
shotgun
should
shoulder
shouldn't
shout
shove
show
shower
shown
showoff

shrank
shred
shrill
shrimp
shrink
shrub
shrug
shrunk
shut
shy
shyly
sick
side
side show
sidewalk
sideways
sift
sigh
sight
sign
silent
silk
silky
sill
silly
simple
sin
since
sinful
sing
singe
singer
single
singular
sink
sip
sir
sister
sisterhood
sit
sitter
six
six-shooter
sixteen
sixty
size
skate
skater
sketch
ski
skid
skill
skillful
skin
skinny
skip
skipper
skirt
skull
skunk

sky
skylight
skyline
skyscraper
slacks
slam
slang
slant
slap
slaughter
slave
sled
sleep
sleepily
sleepless
sleepy
sleet
sleeve
sleeveless
sleigh
slept
slice
slid
slide
slight
slim
sling
slip
slipper
slop
sloppy
slot
slouch
slow
slowdown
slowly
slowpoke
slum
slump
slung
slush
sly
smack
small
smart
smash
smear
smell
smile
Smith
smog
smoggy
smoke
smoker
smoky
smooth
smoothly
smudge
snack
snag

snail
snake
snakebite
snap
snapper
snappy
snapshot
snarl
snatch
sneak
sneakers
sneaky
sneeze
sniff
snip
snob
snore
snow
snowball
snowplow
snowstorm
so
soak
soap
soapy
soar
sob
sock
socks
soda
soft
softly
soil
sold
sole
solid
some
somebody
someone
something
sometimes
somewhat
son
song
soon
sore
sorry
sort
sought
sound
soundly
soup
soupspoon
sour
sourball
sourpuss
south
South America
southpaw
South Pole

southwest
sox
space
spade
spaghetti
Spain
span
spangle
spank
spare
spark
speak
speaker
spear
speck
sped
speech
speechless
speed
speedily
speedy
spell
spelling
spend
spendthrift
spent
spice
spicy
spider
spill
spin
spine
spit
spite
spiteful
splash
spleen
splint
splinter
split
splurge
spoke
spoken
spoil
spoon
spoonful
sponge
spongy
sport
spot
spotless
spout
sprain
sprawl
spray
spread
spring
sprint
sprout
spy

square
squarely
squeak
squeaky
squeal
squeeze
squirm
squirrel
squirt
squish
stadium
stage
stagecoach
stage fright
stain
stair
stairway
stale
stall
stamp
stand
standstill
stank
star
starch
stare
starfish
start
starve
stash
state
statement
station
stay
steak
steal
steam
steel
steep
steer
stem
step
step-by-step
Steve
Steven
stew
stick
sticker
sticky
still
sting
stink
stir
stitch
stocking
stomach
stomp
stone
stony
stood

stool	suds	syllable	thankful	thunder	trader	ulcer
stoop	suffer	tab	Thanksgiving	Thursday	trail	unable
stop	sue	table	that	thus	train	unafraid
store	Sue	tablecloth	that's	tick	trainer	unarmed
stork	sugar	tablespoon	thaw	tide	training	unaware
storm	sugarless	tack	the	tie	trait	uncertain
story	suit	tag	theft	tight	tramp	unclear
stove	suitcase	tail	their	tighten	trance	uncommon
straight	sulk	tailor	them	tightly	trap	uncooked
straighten	sulky	tailspin	themselves	tile	trapper	uncover
strain	sum	take	then	tilt	trash	under
strainer	summer	taken	there	Tim	trashy	underdog
strand	sun	tale	therefore	time	tray	underdone
strange	sunburn	talk	there's	tin	tread	underground
stranger	Sunday	tall	these	tiny	treat	underline
strap	sundown	tame	they	tip	tree	underneath
strapless	sunflower	tan	they're	tire	treeless	undershirt
straw	sung	tank	they've	tissue	trend	understand
strawberry	sunglasses	tap	thick	to	tribe	understood
stray	sunk	tape	thicken	toast	trick	undertaker
streak	sunken	tar	thickly	toaster	tricky	underwear
stream	sunless	task	thief	today		underworld
streamline	sunlight	taste	thin	toe	trim	undid
street	sunny	tasteless	thinner	together	trip	undo
strength	sunrise	tasty	thing	toil	troop	undress
stress	sunset	taught	think	told	trooper	uneasy
stressful	sunshine	tax	thinker	Tom	trouble	uneven
stretch	sunstroke	tea	third	tomato	trounce	unfair
strict	suntan	teach	thirst	Tommy	trousers	unfit
strictly	suppose	teacher	thirsty	tomorrow	trout	unfold
strike	sure	teacup	thirteen	ton	truce	unfriendly
string	surely	team	thirty	tone	truck	unhappy
string bean	surf	teapot	this	tongue	trudge	unhealthy
strip	surprise	tear	Thomas	tonight		unit
stripe	Sutter	tearful	thorn	Tony	true	United States
stroke	swallow	tearoom	those	too	truly	
stroll	swam	tease	though	took	trunk	universe
strong	swamp	teaspoon	thought	tool	trust	unlawful
strongly	swear	Ted	thoughtful	toolbox	truth	unless
struck	sweat	tee	thoughtless	tooth	truthful	unlikely
struggle	sweater	teepee	thousand	toothbrush	truthfully	unluckily
stuck	Swede	teeth	thread	toothpaste	try	unlucky
student	Sweden	television	threat	top	tub	unmade
study	sweep	tell	threaten	topping	tube	unmated
stuff	sweeper	teller	three	tore	tuck	unpack
stuffing	sweet	temper	threw	torn	Tuesday	unsafe
stuffy	swell	temperature	thrift	toss	tug	unsure
stunt	swept	ten	thrifty	total	tune	untie
stupid	swift	tend	thrill	touch		until
stutter	swiftly	tennis	throat	touchdown	tuner	untrained
sub	swim	tenpin	throb	tough	turkey	unwilling
subject	swimmer	tense	throne	toward	turn	unwrap
subway	swing	tent	through	towel	turtle	up
success	swipe	term	throughout	town	TV	up-and-down
successful	swirl	termite	throw	townspeople	twelve	upcoming
successfully	Swiss	terrible	thrown	toy	twenty	update
such	switch	test	thru	trace	twice	uphill
suck	swizzle	Texas	thud	track	twin	upkeep
sudden	sworn	than	thumb	trade	twine	upon
suddenly	swung	thank	thump		twist	upper
					two	
					ugly	